"WAITING ON GOD"

A 31 Day Devotional

Andrew Murray

ISBN-13:
978-1502486240

ISBN-10:
1502486245

Contents

PREFACE

PREVIOUS to my leaving for England last year, I had been much impressed by the thought of how, in all our religion, personal and public, we need more of God. I had felt that we needed to train our people in their worship more to wait on God, and to make the cultivation of a deeper sense of His presence, of more direct contact with Him, of entire dependence on Him, a definite aim of our ministry. At a 'welcome' breakfast in Exeter Hall, I gave very simple expression to this thought in connection with all our religious work. I have already said elsewhere that I was surprised at the response the sentiment met with. I saw that God's Spirit had been working the same desire in many hearts.

The experiences of the past year, both personal and public, have greatly deepened the conviction. It is as if I myself am only beginning to see the deepest truth concerning God, and our relation to Him, center in this waiting on God, and how very little, in our life and work, we have been surrounded by its spirit. The following pages are the outcome of my conviction, and of the desire to direct the attention of all God's people to the one great remedy for all our needs. More than half the pieces were written on board ship; I fear they bear the marks of being somewhat crude and hasty. I have felt, in looking them over, as if I could wish to write them over again. But this I cannot now do. And so I send them out with the prayer that He who loves to use the feeble may give His blessing with them.

I do not know if it will be possible for me to put into a few words what are the chief things we need to learn. In a note at the close of the book on Law I have mentioned some. But what I want to say here is this: The great lack of our religion is, we do not know God. The answer to every complaint of feebleness and failure, the message to every congregation or convention seeking instruction on holiness, ought to be simply, What is the matter: Have you not God? If you really believe in God, He will put all right. God is willing and able by His Holy Spirit. Cease from expecting the least good from yourself, or the least help from anything there is in man, and just yield yourself unreservedly to God to work in you: He will do all for you.

How simple this looks! And yet this is the gospel we so little know. I feel ashamed as I send forth these very defective meditations; I can only cast them on the love of my brethren, and of our God. May He use them to draw us all to Himself, to learn in practice and experience the blessed art of Waiting only upon God. Would God that we might get some right conception of what the influence would be of a life given, not in thought, or imagination, or effort, but in the power of the Holy Spirit, wholly to waiting upon God.

With my greeting in Christ to all God's saints it has been my privilege to meet, and no less to those I have not met, I subscribe myself, your brother and servant,

ANDREW MURRAY.
Wellington
3rd March 1896

First Day. *WAITING ON GOD: The God of Our Salvation.*

'My soul waiteth only upon God [margin: is silent unto God]; from Him cometh my salvation.'--Ps. 62: 1(R.V.).

IF salvation indeed comes from God, and is entirely His work, just as our creation was, it follows, as a matter of course, that our first and highest duty is to wait on Him to do that work as it pleases Him. Waiting becomes then the only way to the experience of a full salvation, the only way, truly, to know God as the God of our salvation. All the difficulties that are brought forward as keeping us back from full salvation, have their cause in this one thing: the defective knowledge and practice of waiting upon God. All that the Church and its members need for the manifestation of the mighty power of God in the world, is the return to our true place, the place that belongs to us, both in creation and redemption, the place of absolute and unceasing dependence upon God. Let us strive to see what the elements are that make up this most blessed and needful waiting upon God: it may help us to discover the reasons why this grace is so little cultivated, and to feel how infinitely desirable it is that the Church, that we ourselves, should at any price learn its blessed secret.

The deep need for this waiting on God lies equally in the nature of man and the nature of God. God, as Creator, formed man, to be a vessel in which He could show forth His power and goodness. Man was not to have in himself a

3

fountain of life, or strength, or happiness: the ever living and only living One was each moment to be the Communicator to him of all that he needed. Man's glory and blessedness was not to be independent, or dependent upon himself, but dependent on a God of such infinite riches and love. Man was to have the joy of receiving every moment out of the fulness of God. This was his blessedness as an unfallen creature.

When he fell from God, he was still more absolutely dependent on Him. There was not the slightest hope of his recovery out of his state of death, but in God, His power and mercy. It is God alone who began the work of redemption; it is God alone who continues and carries it on each moment in each individual believer. Even in the regenerate man there is no power of goodness in himself: he has and can have nothing that he does not each moment receive; and waiting on God is just as indispensable, and must be just as continuous and unbroken, as the breathing that maintains his natural life.

It is, then, because Christians do not know in their relation to God of their own absolute poverty and helplessness, that they have no sense of the need of absolute and unceasing dependence, or of the unspeakable blessedness of continual waiting on God. But when once a believer begins to see it, and consent to it, that he by the Holy Spirit must each moment receive what God each moment works, waiting on God becomes his brightest hope and joy. As he appreciates how God, as God, as Infinite Love, delights to impart His own nature to His child as fully as He can, how God is not weary of each moment keeping charge of his life and strength, he wonders that he ever thought otherwise of God than as a God to be waited on all the day. God unceasingly giving and working; His child unceasingly waiting and receiving: this is the blessed life.

'Truly my soul waiteth upon God; from Him cometh my salvation.' First we wait on God for salvation. Then we learn that salvation is only to bring us to God, and teach us to wait on Him. Then we find what is better still, that waiting on God is itself the highest salvation. It is the ascribing to Him the glory of being All; it is the experiencing that He is All to us. May God teach us the blessedness of waiting on Him.

'My soul, wait thou only upon God!'

Second Day. *WAITING ON GOD: The Keynote of Life.*

'I have waited for Thy salvation, O Lord!'--Gen. 49: 18.

IT is not easy to say exactly in what sense Jacob used these words, in the midst of his prophecies in regard to the future of his sons. But they do certainly indicate that both for himself and for them his expectation was from God alone. It was God's salvation he waited for; a salvation which God had promised and which God Himself alone could work out. He knew himself and his sons to be under God's charge. Jehovah the Everlasting God would show in them what His saving power is and does. The words point forward to that wonderful history of redemption which is not yet finished, and to the glorious future in eternity. They suggest to us how there is no salvation but God's salvation, and how waiting on God for that, whether for our personal experience, or in wider circles, is our first duty, our true blessedness.

Let us think of ourselves, and the inconceivably glorious salvation God has wrought for us in Christ, and is now purposing to work out and to perfect in us by His Spirit. Let us meditate until we somewhat realize that every participation of this great salvation, from moment to moment, must be the work of God Himself. God cannot part with His grace, or goodness, or strength, as an external thing that He gives us, as He gives the raindrops from heaven. No; He can only give it, and we can only enjoy it, as He works it Himself directly and unceasingly. And the only reason that He does not work it more effectively and continuously is, that we do not let Him. We hinder Him either by our indifference or by our self-effort, so that He cannot do what He would. What He asks of us, in the way of surrender, and obedience, and desire, and trust, is all comprised in this one word: waiting on Him, waiting for His salvation. It combines the deep sense of our entire helplessness of ourselves to work what is divinely good, and the perfect confidence that our God will work it all in His divine power.

Again, I say, let us meditate on the divine glory of the salvation God purposes working out in us, until we know the truth it implies. Our heart is the scene of a divine operation more wonderful than Creation. We can do as little towards the work as towards creating the world, except as God works in us to will and to do. God only asks of us to yield, to consent, to wait upon Him, and He will do it all. Let us meditate and be still, until we see how appropriate and right and blessed it is that God alone do all, and our soul will of itself sink down in deep humility to say: 'I have waited for Thy salvation, O Lord.' And the deep blessed background of all our praying and working will be: 'Truly my soul waiteth upon God.'

The application of the truth to wider circles, to those we labor among or intercede for, to the Church of Christ around us, or throughout the world, is not difficult. There can be no good but what God works; to wait upon God, and have the heart filled with faith in His working, and in that faith to pray for His mighty power to come down, is our only wisdom. Oh for the eyes of our heart to be opened to see God working in ourselves and in others, and to see how blessed it is to worship and just to wait for His salvation!

Our private and public prayer are our chief expression of our relation to God: it is in them chiefly that our waiting upon God must be exercised. If our waiting begin by quieting the activities of nature, and being still before God; if it bows and seeks to see God in His universal and almighty operation, alone able and always ready to work all good; if it yields itself to Him in the assurance that He is working and will work in us; if it maintains the place of humility and stillness and surrender, until God's Spirit has quickened the faith that He will perfect His work: it will indeed become the strength and the joy of the soul. Life will become one deep blessed cry: 'I have waited for Thy salvation, O Lord.'

'My soul, wait thou only upon God!'

Third Day. *WAITING ON GOD: The True Place of the Creature.*

'These wait all upon Thee;

That Thou mayest give them their meat in due season.

That Thou givest unto them, they gather;

Thou openest Thine hand, they are satisfied with good.

Ps. 104:27, 28(R.V.).

THIS Psalm, in praise of the Creator, has been speaking of the birds and the beasts of the forest; of the young lions, and man going forth to his work; of the great sea, wherein are things creeping innumerable, both small and great beasts. And it sums up the whole relation of all creation to its Creator, and its continuous and universal dependence upon Him in the one word: 'These all wait upon Thee!' Just as much as it was God's work to create, it is His work to maintain. As little as the creature could create itself, is it left to provide for itself. The whole creation is ruled by the one unalterable law of--waiting upon God!

The word is the simple expression of that for the sake of which alone the creature was brought into existence, the very groundwork of its constitution. The one object for which God gave life to creatures was that in them He might prove and show forth His wisdom, power, and goodness, inHis being each moment their life and happiness, and pouring forth unto them, according to their capacity, the riches of his goodness and power. And just as this is the very place and nature of God, to be unceasingly the supplier of every want in the creature, so the very place and nature of the creature is nothing but this--to wait upon God and receive from Him what He alone can give, what He delights to give. (See note on Law, The Power of the Spirit.)

If we are in this little book at all to appreciate what waiting on God is to be to the believer, to practice it and to experience its blessedness, it is of consequence that we begin at the very beginning, and see the deep reasonableness of the call that comes to us. We shall understand how the duty is no arbitrary command. We shall see how it is not only rendered necessary by our sin and helplessness. It is simply and truly our restoration to our original destiny and our highest nobility, to our true place and glory as creatures blessedly dependent on the All-Glorious God.

If once our eyes are opened to this precious truth, all Nature will become a preacher, reminding us of the relationship which, founded in creation, is now taken up in grace. As we read this Psalm, and learn to look upon all life in Nature as continually maintained by God Himself, waiting on God will be seen to be the very necessity of our being. As we think of the young lions and the ravens crying to Him, of the birds and the fish and every insect waiting on Him, until He give them their meat in due season, we shall see that it is the very nature and glory of God that He is a God who is to be waited on. Every thought of what Nature is, and what God is, will give new force to the call:

'Wait thou only upon God.'

'These all wait upon Thee, that thou may give.' It is God who gives all: let this faith enter deeply into our hearts. Ere yet we fully understand all that is implied in our waiting upon God, and ere we ever have been able to cultivate the habit, let the truth enter our souls: waiting on God, unceasing and entire dependence upon Him, is, in heaven and earth, the one only true religion, the one unalterable and all-comprehensive expression for the true relationship to the ever-blessed One in whom we live.

Let us resolve at once that it shall be the one characteristic of our life and worship, a continual, humble, trustful waiting upon God. We may rest assured that He who made us for Himself, that He might give Himself to us and in us, that He will never disappoint us. In waiting on Him we shall find rest and joy and strength, and the supply of every need.

'My soul, wait thou only upon God!'

Fourth Day. *WAITING ON GOD: For Supplies.*

'The Lord upholdeth all that fall,

And raiseth up all those that be bowed down.

The eyes of all wait upon Thee;

And Thou givest them their meat in due season.'

--Ps. 145:14, 15.

PSALM 104 is a Psalm of Creation, and the words, 'These all wait upon Thee,' were used with reference to the animal creation. Here we have a Psalm of the Kingdom, and 'The eyes of all wait upon Thee' appears especially to point to the needs of God's saints, of all that fall and them that be bowed down. What the universe and the animal creation does unconsciously, God's people are to do intelligently and voluntarily. Man is to be the interpreter of Nature. He is to prove that there is nothing more noble or more blessed in the exercise of our free will than to use it in waiting upon God.

If an army has been sent out to march into an enemy's country, and tidings are received that it is not advancing, the question is at once asked, what may be the cause of delay. The answer will very often be: 'Waiting for supplies.' All the stores of provisions or clothing or ammunition have not arrived; without these it dare not proceed. It is no otherwise in the Christian life: day by day, at every step, we need our supplies from above. And there is nothing so needful as to cultivate that spirit of dependence on God and of confidence in Him, which refuses to go on without the needed supply of grace and strength.

If the question be asked, whether this be anything different from what we do when we pray, the answer is, that there may be much praying with but very little waiting on God. In praying we are often occupied with ourselves, with our own needs, and our own efforts in the presentation of them. In waiting upon God, the first thought is of the God upon whom we wait. We enter His presence, and feel we need just to be quiet, so that He, as God, can overshadow us with Himself. God longs to reveal Himself, to fill us with Himself. Waiting on God gives Him time in His own way and divine power to come to us.

It is especially at the time of prayer that we ought to set ourselves to cultivate this spirit.

Prayer

Before you pray, bow quietly before God, just to remember and realize who He is, how near He is, how certainly He can and will help. Just be still before Him, and allow His Holy Spirit to waken and stir up in your soul the childlike disposition of absolute dependence and confident expectation. Wait upon God as a Living Being, as the Living God, who notices you, and is just longing to fill you with His salvation. Wait on God until you know you have met Him; prayer will then become so different.

Silence

And when you are praying, let there be intervals of silence, reverent stillness of soul, in which you yield yourself to God, in case He may have aught He wishes to teach you or to work in you. Waiting on Him will become the most blessed part of prayer, and the blessing thus obtained will be doubly precious as the fruit of such fellowship with the Holy One. God has so ordained it, in harmony with His holy nature, and with ours, that waiting on Him should be the honor we give Him. Let us bring Him the service gladly and truthfully; He will reward it abundantly.

'The eyes of all wait upon Thee, and Thou givest them their meat in due season.' Dear soul, God provides in Nature for the creatures He has made: how much more will He provide in Grace for those He has redeemed. Learn to say of every want, and every failure, and every lack of needful grace: I have waited too little upon God, or He would have given me in due season all I needed. And say then too-

'My soul, wait thou only upon God!'

Fifth Day.*WAITING ON GOD: For Instruction.*

'Shew me thy ways, O Lord; Teach me Thy paths.

Teach me Thy paths.

Lead me in Thy truth, and teach me;

For Thou art the God of my salvation;

On Thee do I wait all the day.'-- Ps. 25:4, 5. 'I SPOKE of an army, on the point of entering an enemy's territories, answering the question as to the cause of delay: 'Waiting for supplies.' The answer might also have been: 'Waiting for instructions,' or, 'Waiting for orders.' If the last despatch had not been received, with the final orders of the commander-in-chief, the army dared not move. Even so in the Christian life: as deep as the need of waiting for supplies, is that of waiting for instructions.'

See how beautifully this comes out in Ps. 25. The writer knew and loved God's law exceedingly, and meditated in that law day and night. But he knew that this was not enough. He knew that for the right spiritual apprehension of the truth, and for the right personal application of it to his own peculiar circumstances, he needed a direct divine teaching.

The psalm has at all times been a very favourite one, because of its reiterated expression of the felt need of the Divine teaching, and of the childlike confidence that that teaching would be given. Study the psalm until your heart is filled with the two thoughts--the absolute need, the absolute certainty of divine guidance. And notice, then, how entirely it is in this connection that he speaks, On Thee do I wait all the day.' Waiting for guidance, waiting for instruction, all the day, is a very blessed part of waiting upon God.

The Father in heaven is so interested in His child, and so longs to have his life at every step in His will and His love, that He is willing to keep his guidance entirely in His own hand. He knows so well that we are unable to do what is really holy and heavenly, except as He works it in us, that He means His very demands to become promises of what He will do, in watching over and leading us all the day. Not only in special difficulties and times of perplexity, but in the common course of everyday life, we may count upon Him to teach us His way, and show us His path.

And what is needed in us to receive this guidance? One thing: waiting for instructions, waiting on God. 'On Thee do I wait all the day.' We want in our times of prayer to give clear expression to our sense of need, and our faith in His help. We want definitely to become conscious of our ignorance as to what God's way may be, and the need of the Divine light shining within us, if our way is to be as of the sun, shining more and more unto the perfect day. And we want to wait quietly before God in prayer, until the deep, restful assurance fills us: It will be given--'the meek will He guide in the way.' 'On Thee do I wait all the day.' The special surrender to the Divine guidance in our seasons of prayer must cultivate, and be followed up by, the habitual looking upwards 'all the day.' As simple as it is, to one who has eyes, to walk all the day in the light of the sun, so simple and delightful can it become to a soul practiced in waiting on God, to walk all the day in the enjoyment of God's light and leading. What is needed to help us to such a life is just one thing: the real knowledge and faith of God as the one only source of wisdom and goodness, as ever ready, and longing much to be to us all that we can possibly require--yes! this is the one thing we need. If we but saw our God in His love, if we but believed that He waits to be gracious, that He waits to be our life and to work all in us,--how this waiting on God would become our highest joy, the natural and spontaneous response of our hearts to His great love and glory!

'My soul, wait thou only upon God!'

Sixth Day.*WAITING ON GOD: For all Saints.*

'Let none that wait on Thee be ashamed.'-- Ps. 25:3

LET us now, in our meditation of today, each one forget himself, to think of the great company of God's saints throughout the world, who are all with us waiting on Him. And let us all join in the fervent prayer for each other, 'Let none that wait on Thee be ashamed.'

Just think for a moment of the multitude of waiting ones who need that prayer; how many there are, sick and weary and solitary, to whom it is as if their prayers are not answered, and who sometimes begin to fear that their hope will be put to shame. And then, how many servants of God, ministers or missionaries, teachers or workers, of various name, whose hopes in their work have been disappointed, and whose longing for power and blessing remains unsatisfied. And then, too, how many, who have heard of a life of rest and perfect peace, of abiding light and fellowship, of strength and victory, and who cannot find the path. With all these, it is nothing but that they have not yet learned the secret of full waiting upon God. They just need, what we all need, the living assurance that waiting on God can never be in vain. Let us remember all who are in danger of fainting or being weary, and all unite in the cry, 'Let none that wait on Thee be ashamed'!

If this intercession for all who wait on God becomes part of our waiting on Him for ourselves, we shall help to bear each other's burdens, and so fulfil the law of Christ.

There will be introduced into our waiting on God that

element of unselfishness and love, which is the path to the highest blessing, and the fullest communion with God. Love to the brethren and love to God are inseparably linked. In God, the love to His Son and to us are one: 'That the love wherewith Thou hast loved Me, may be in them.' In Christ, the love of the Father to Him, and His love to us, are one: 'As the Father loved me, so have I loved you.' In us, He asks that His love to us shall be ours to the brethren: 'As I have loved you, that ye love one another.' All the love of God, and of Christ, are inseparably linked with love to the brethren. And how can we, day by day, prove and cultivate this love otherwise than by daily praying for each other? Christ did not seek to enjoy the Father's love for Himself; He passed it all on to us. All true seeking of God and His love for ourselves, will be inseparably linked with the thought and the love of our brethren in prayer for them.

'Let none that wait on Thee be ashamed.' Twice in the psalm David speaks of his waiting on God for himself; here he thinks of all who wait on Him. Let this page take the message to all God's tried and weary ones, that there are more praying for them than they know. Let it stir them and us in our waiting to make a point of at times forgetting ourselves, and to enlarge our hearts, and say to the Father, 'These all wait upon Thee, and Thou givest them their meat in due season.' Let it inspire us all with new courage--for who is there who is not at times ready to faint and be weary? 'Let none that wait on Thee be ashamed' is a promise in a prayer, 'They that wait on Thee shall not be ashamed'! From many and many a witness the cry comes to everyone who needs the help, brother, sister, tried one, 'Wait on the Lord; be of good courage, and He shall strengthen your heart; wait, I say, on the Lord. Be of good courage, and He shall strengthen your heart, all ye that wait on the Lord.'

Blessed Father! we humbly beseech Thee, Let none that wait on Thee be ashamed; no, not one. Some are weary, and the time of waiting appears long. And some are feeble, and scarcely know how to wait. And some are so entangled in the effort of their prayers and their work, they think that they can find no time to wait continually. Father! teach us all how to wait. Teach us to think of each other, and pray for each other. Teach us to think of Thee, the God of all waiting ones. Father! let none that wait on Thee be ashamed. For Jesus' sake. Amen.

'My soul, wait thou only upon God!'

Seventh Day. *WAITING ON GOD: A Plea in Prayer.*

'Let integrity and uprightness preserve me; for I wait on Thee.'-- Ps. 25:21

FOR the third time in this psalm we have the word wait. As before in ver. 5, 'On Thee do I wait all the day,' so here, too, the believing supplicant appeals to God to remember that he is waiting on Him, looking for an answer. It is a great thing for a soul not only to wait upon God, but to be filled with such a consciousness that its whole spirit and position is that of a waiting one, that it can, in childlike confidence, say, Lord! Thou knowest, I wait on Thee. It will prove a mighty plea in prayer, giving ever-increasing boldness of expectation to claim the promise, 'They that wait on Me shall not be ashamed'!

The prayer in connection with which the plea is put forth here is one of great importance in the spiritual life. If we draw near to God, it must be with a true heart. There must be perfect integrity, wholeheartedness, in our dealing with God. As we read in the next Psalm (26: 1, 11), 'Judge me, O Lord, for I have walked in my integrity,' 'As for me, I will walk in my integrity,' there must be perfect uprightness or single-heartedness before God. As it is written, 'His righteousness is for the upright in heart.' The soul must know that it allows nothing sinful, nothing doubtful; if it is indeed to meet the Holy One, and receive His full blessing, it must be with a heart wholly and singly given up to His will. The whole spirit that animates us in the waiting must be, 'Let integrity and uprightness'--Thou seest that I desire to come so to Thee, You know I am looking to Thee to work them perfectly in me;--let them 'preserve me, for I wait on Thee.'

And if at our first attempt truly to live the life of fully and always waiting on God, we begin to discover how much that perfect integrity is wanting, this will just be one of the blessings which the waiting was meant to work. A soul cannot seek close fellowship with God, or attain the abiding consciousness of waiting on Him all the day, without a very honest and entire surrender to all His will.

'For I wait on Thee': it is not only in connection with the prayer of our text but with every prayer that this plea may be used. To use it often will be a great blessing to ourselves. Let us therefore study the words well until we know all their bearings. It must be clear to us what we are waiting for. There may be very different things. It may be waiting for God in our times of prayer to take his place as God, and to work in us the sense of His holy presence and nearness. It may be some special petition, to which we are expecting an answer. It may be our whole inner life, in which we are on the lookout for God's putting forth of His power. It may be the whole state of His Church and saints, or some part of His work, for which our eyes are ever toward Him. It is good that we sometimes count up to ourselves exactly what the things are we are waiting for, and as we say definitely of each of them, 'On Thee do I wait,' we shall be emboldened to claim the answer, 'For on Thee do I wait.'

It must also be clear to us, on Whom we are waiting. Not an idol, a God of whom we have made an image by our conceptions of what He is. No, but the living God, such as He really is in His great glory, His infinite holiness, His power, wisdom, and goodness, in His love and nearness. Itis the presence of a beloved or a dreaded master that wakens up the whole attention of the servant who waits on him. It is the presence of God, as He can in Christ by His Holy Spirit make Himself known, and keep the soul under its covering and shadow, that will awaken and strengthen the true waiting spirit. Let us be still and wait and worship until we know how near He is, and then say, 'On Thee do I wait.'

And then, let it be very clear, too, that we are waiting. Let that become so much our consciousness that the utterance comes spontaneously, 'On Thee I do wait all the day; I wait on Thee.' This will indeed imply sacrifice and separation, a soul entirely given up to God as its all, its only joy. This waiting on God has hardly yet been acknowledged as the only true Christianity. And yet, if it be true that God alone is goodness and joy and love; if it be true that our highest blessedness is in having as much of God as we can; if it be true that Christ has redeemed us wholly for God, and made a life of continual abiding in His presence possible, nothing less ought to satisfy than to be ever breathing this blessed atmosphere, 'I wait on Thee.'

'My soul, wait thou only upon God!'

Eighth Day.*WAITING ON GOD: Strong and of Good Courage.*

'Wait on the Lord: be strong, And let your heart take courage:

Yea, wait thou on the Lord.'-- Ps. 27:14 (R.V.)

THE psalmist had just said, 'I had fainted, unless I had believed to see the goodness of the Lord in the land of the living.' If it had not been for his faith in God, his heart had fainted. But in the confident assurance in God which faith gives, he urges himself and us to remember one thing above all,--to wait upon God. 'Wait on the Lord: be strong, and let your heart take courage: yea, wait on the Lord.' One of the chief needs in our waiting upon God, one of the deepest secrets of its blessedness and blessing, is a quiet, confident persuasion that it is not in vain; courage to believe that God will hear and help; that we are waiting on a God who never could disappoint His people.

'Be strong and of good courage.' These words are frequently found in connection with some great and difficult enterprise, in prospect of the combat with the power of strong enemies, and the utter insufficiency of all human strength. Is waiting on God a work so difficult, that, for that too, such words are needed, 'Be strong, and let your heart take courage'? Yes, indeed. The deliverance, for which we often have to wait, is from enemies, in presence of whom we are impotent. The blessings for which we plead are spiritual and all unseen; things impossible with men; heavenly, supernatural, divine realities. Our souls are so little accustomed to hold fellowship with God, the God on whom we wait so often appears to hide Himself. We who have to wait are often tempted to fear that we do not wait aright, that our faith is too feeble, that our desire is not as upright or as earnest as it should be, that our surrender is not complete. Our heart may well faint and fail. Amid all these causes of fear or doubt, how blessed to hear the voice of God, Wait on the Lord! Be strong, and let your heart take courage! Yea, wait thou upon the Lord! Let nothing in heaven or earth or hell--let nothing keep you from waiting on your God in full assurance that it cannot be in vain.

The one lesson our text teaches us is thus, that when we set ourselves to wait on God, we ought beforehand to resolve that it shall be with the most confident expectation of God's meeting and blessing us. We ought to make up our minds to this, that nothing was ever so sure, as that waiting on God will bring us untold and unexpected blessing. We are so accustomed to judge of God and His work in us by what we feel, that the great probability is that when we begin more to cultivate the waiting on Him, we shall be discouraged, because we do not find any special blessing from it. The message comes to us, 'Above everything, when you wait on God, do so in the spirit of abounding hopefulness. It is God in His glory, in His power, in His love longing to bless you that you are waiting on.'

If you say that you are afraid of deceiving yourself with vain hope, because you do not see or feel any warrant in your present state for such special expectations, my answer is, it is God, who is the warrant for your expecting great things. Oh, do learn the lesson. You are not going to wait on yourself to see what you feel and what changes come to you. You are going to WAIT ON GOD, to know first, WHAT HE IS, and then, after that, what He will do. The whole duty and blessedness of waiting on God has its root in this, that He is such a blessed Being, full, to overflowing, of goodness and power and life and joy, that we, however wretched, cannot for any time come into contact with Him, without that life and power secretly, silently beginning to enter into us and blessing us. God is Love! That is the one only and allsufficient warrant of your expectation. Love seeks not its own: God's love is just His delight to impart Himself and His blessedness to His children. Come, and however feeble you feel, just wait in His presence. As a feeble, sickly invalid is brought out into the sunshine to let its warmth go through him, come with all that is dark and cold in you into the sunshine of God's holy, omnipotent love, and sit and wait there, with the one thought: Here I am, in the sunshine of His love. As the sun does its work in the weak one who seeks its rays, God will do His work in you. Oh, do trust Him fully. 'Wait on the Lord! Be strong, and let your heart take courage! Yea, wait on the Lord'!

'My soul, wait thou only upon God!'

Ninth Day. *WAITING ON GOD: With the Heart.*

'Be strong, and let your heart take courage,

All ye that wait for the Lord.'-- Ps. 31: 24. (R.V.)

THE words are nearly the same as in our last meditation. But I gladly avail myself of them again to press home a much-needed lesson for all who desire to learn truly and fully what waiting on God is. The lesson is this: It is with the heart we must wait upon God. 'Let your heart take courage.' All our waiting depends upon the state of the heart. As a man's heart is, so is he before God. We can advance no further or deeper into the holy place of God's presence to wait on Him there, than our heart is prepared for it by the Holy Spirit. The message is, 'Let your heart take courage, all you that wait on the Lord.'

The truth appears so simple, that some may ask, Do not all admit this? where is the need of insisting on it so specially? Because very many Christians have no sense of the great difference between the religion of the mind and the religion of the heart, and the former is far more diligently cultivated than the latter. They know not how infinitely greater the heart is than the mind. It is in this that one of the chief causes must be sought of the feebleness of our Christian life, and it is only as this is understood that waiting on God will bring its full blessing.

Proverbs 3: 5 may help to make my meaning plain. Speaking of a life in the fear and favor of God, it says, 'Trust in the Lord with all your heart, and lean not upon your own understanding.' In all religion we have to use these two powers. The mind has to gather knowledge from God's word, and prepare the food by which the heart with the inner life is to be nourished. But here comes in a terrible danger, of our leaning to our own understanding, and trusting in our understanding of divine things. People imagine that if they are occupied with the truth, the spiritual life will as a matter of course be strengthened. And this is by no means the case. The understanding deals with conceptions and images of divine things, but it cannot reach the real life of the soul. Hence the command, 'Trust in the Lord with all your heart, and lean not upon your own understanding.' It is with the heart man believes, and comes into touch with God. It is in the heart God has given His Spirit, to be there to us the presence and the power of God working in us. In all our religion it is the heart that must trust and love and worship and obey. My mind is utterly impotent in creating or maintaining the spiritual life within me: the heart must wait on God for Him to work it in me.

It is in this even as in the physical life. My reason may tell me what to eat and drink, and how the food nourishes me. But in the eating and feeding my reason can do nothing: the body has its organs for that special purpose. Just so, reason may tell me what God's word says, but it can do nothing to the feeding of the soul on the bread of life--this the heart alone can do by its faith and trust in God. A man may be studying the nature and effects of food or sleep; when he wants to eat or sleep he sets aside his thoughts and study, and uses the power of eating or sleeping. And so the Christian needs ever, when he has studied or heard

God's word, to cease from his thoughts, to put no trust in them, and to awaken his heart to open itself before God, and seek the living fellowship with Him.

This is now the blessedness of waiting upon God, that I confess the impotence of all my thoughts and efforts, and set myself still to bow my heart before Him in holy silence, and to trust Him to renew and strengthen His own work in me. And this is just the lesson of our text, 'Let your heart take courage, all you that wait on the Lord.' Remember the difference between knowing with the mind and believing with the heart. Beware of the temptation of leaning upon your understanding, with its clear strong thoughts. They only help you to know what the heart must get from God: in themselves they are only images and shadows. 'Let your heart take courage, all ye that wait on the Lord.' Present it before Him as that wonderful part of your spiritual nature in which God reveals Himself, and by which you can know Him. Cultivate the greatest confidence that, though you cannot see into your heart, God is working there by His Holy Spirit. Let the heart wait at times in perfect silence and quiet; in its hidden depths God will work. Be sure of this, and just wait on Him. Give your whole heart, with its secret workings, into God's hands continually. He wants the heart, and takes it, and as God dwells in it. 'Be strong, and let your heart take courage, all ye that wait on the Lord.'

'My soul, wait thou only upon God!'

Tenth Day. *WAITING FOR GOD: In Humble Fear and Hope.*

'Behold, the eye of the Lord is upon them that fear Him,

Upon them that hope in His mercy;

To deliver their soul from death,

And to keep them alive in famine.

Our soul hath waited for the Lord;

He is our help and our shield.

For our heart shall rejoice in Him,

Because we have trusted in His holy name. Let thy mercy, O Lord, be upon us,

According as we wait for thee.'

--Ps. 33:18-22(R.V.).

GOD'S eye is upon His people: their eye is upon Him. In waiting upon God, our eye, looking up to Him, meets His looking down upon us. This is the blessedness of waiting upon God, that it takes our eyes and thoughts away from ourselves, even our needs and desires, and occupies us with our God. We worship Him in His glory and love, with His all-seeing eye watching over us, that He may supply our every need. Let us consider this wonderful meeting between God and His people, and mark well what we are taught here of those on whom God's eye rests, and of Him on whom our eye rests.

'The eye of the Lord is on them that fear Him, on them that hope in His mercy.' Fear and hope are generally thought to be in conflict with each other; in the presence and worship of God they are found side by side in perfect and beautiful harmony. And this because in God Himself all apparent contradictions are reconciled. Righteousness and peace, judgment and mercy, holiness and love, infinite power and infinite gentleness, a majesty that is exalted above all heaven, and a condescension that bows very low, meet and kiss each other. There is indeed a fear that has torment, that is cast out entirely by perfect love. But there is a fear that is found in the very heavens. In the song of Moses and the Lamb they sing, 'Who shall not fear Thee, O Lord, and glorify Thy name?' And out of the very throne the voice came, 'Praise our God, all His servants, and ye that fear Him.' Let us in our waiting ever seek 'to fear the glorious and fearful name, The Lord thy God.' The deeper we bow before His holiness in holy fear and adoring awe, in deep reverence and humble self-abasement, even as the angels veil their faces before the throne, the more will His holiness rest upon us, and the soul be fitted to have God reveal Himself; the deeper we enter into the truth 'that no flesh glory in His presence,' will it be given us to see His glory. 'The eye of the Lord is on them that fear Him.'

'On them that hope in His mercy.' So far will the true fear of God be from keeping us back from hope, it will stimulate and strengthen it. The lower we bow, the deeper we feel we have nothing to hope in but His mercy. The lower we bow, the nearer God will come, and make our hearts bold to trust Him. Let every exercise of waiting, let our whole habit of waiting on God, be pervaded by abounding hope--a hope as bright and boundless as God's mercy. The fatherly kindness of God is such that, in whatever state we come to Him, we may confidently hope in His mercy.

Such are God's waiting ones. And now, think of the God on whom we wait. 'The eye of the Lordis on them that fear Him, on them that hope in His mercy; to deliver their soul from death, and to keep them alive in famine.' Not to prevent the danger of death and famine--this is often needed to stir up to wait on Him--but to deliver and to keep alive. For the dangers are often very real and dark; the situation, whether in the temporal or spiritual life, may appear to be utterly hopeless; there is always one hope: God's eye is on them.

That eye sees the danger, and sees in tender love His trembling waiting child, and sees the moment when the heart is ripe for the blessing, and sees the way in which it is to come. This living, mighty God, oh, let us fear Him and hope in His mercy. And let us humbly but boldly say, 'Our soul waiteth for the Lord; He is our help and our shield. Let Thy mercy be upon us, O Lord, according as we wait for Thee.'

Oh, the blessedness of waiting on such a God! a very present help in every time of trouble; a shield and defense against every danger. Children of God! will you not learn to sink down in entire helplessness and impotence, and in stillness to wait and see the salvation of God? In the utmost spiritual famine, and when death appears to prevail, oh, wait on God. He does deliver, He does keep alive. Say it not only in solitude, but say it to each other-- the psalm speaks not of one but of God's people--'Our soul waits on the Lord: He is our help and our shield.' Strengthen and encourage each other in the holy exercise of waiting, that each may not only say it of himself, but of his brethren, 'We have waited for Him; we will be glad and rejoice in His salvation.'

'My soul, wait thou only upon God!'

Eleventh Day. *WAITING ON GOD: Patiently.*

'Rest in the Lord, and wait patiently for Him.

Those that wait upon the Lord, they shall inherit the land.'--Ps. 37: 7,9(R.V.).

'IN patience possess your souls.' 'Ye have need of patience.' 'Let patience have its perfect work, that ye may be perfect and entire.' Such words of the Holy Spirit show us what an important element in the Christian life and character patience is. And nowhere is there a better place for cultivating or displaying it than in waiting on God. There we discover how impatient we are, and what our impatience means. We confess at times that we are impatient with men and circumstances that hinder us, or with ourselves and our slow progress in the Christian life. If we truly set ourselves to wait upon God, we shall find that it is with Him we are impatient, because He does not at once, or as soon as we could wish, do our bidding. It is in waiting upon God that our eyes are opened to believe in His wise and sovereign will, and to see that the sooner and the more completely we yield absolutely to it, the more surely His blessing can come to us.

'It is not of him that wills, nor of him that runs, but of God that shows mercy.' We have as little power to increase or strengthen our spiritual life, as we had to originate it. We 'were born not of the will of the flesh, nor of the will of man, but of the will of God.' Even so, our willing and running, our desire and effort, avail nought; all is 'of God that showeth mercy.' All the exercises of the spiritual life,

our reading and praying, our willing and doing, have their
very great value. But they can go no farther than this, that
they point the way and prepare us in humility to look to
and to depend alone upon God Himself, and in patience to
await His good time and mercy. The waiting is to teach us
our absolute dependence upon God's mighty working, and
to make us in perfect patience place ourselves at His
disposal. They that wait on the Lord shall inherit the land;
the promised land and its blessing. The heirs must wait;
they can afford to wait.

'Rest in the lord, and wait patiently for Him.' The margin
gives for 'Rest in the Lord,' 'Be silent to the Lord,' or R.V.,
'Be still before the Lord.' It is resting in the Lord, in His will,
His promise, His faithfulness, and His love, that makes
patience easy. And the resting in Him is nothing but being
silent unto Him, still before Him. Having our thoughts and
wishes, our fears and hopes, hushed into calm and quiet in
that great peace of God which passeth all understanding.
That peace keeps the heart and mind when we are anxious
for anything, because we have made our request known to
Him. The rest, the silence, the stillness, and the patient
waiting, all find their strength and joy in God Himself.

The needs be, and the reasonableness, and the
blessedness of patience will be opened up to the waiting
soul. Our patience will be seen to be the counterpart of
God's patience. He longs far more to bless us fully than we
can desire it. But, as the husbandman has long patience
until the fruit be ripe, so God bows Himself to our
slowness and bears long with us. Let us remember this,
and wait patiently: of each promise and every answer to

prayer the word is true: 'I the Lord will hasten it in its time.'

'Rest in the Lord, and wait patiently for Him.' Yes, for Him. Seek not only the help, the gift, you need; seek Himself; wait for Him. Give God His glory by resting in Him, by trusting him fully, by waiting patiently for Him. This patience honors Him greatly; it leaves Him, as God on the throne, to do His work; it yields self wholly into His hands. It lets God be God. If your waiting be for some special request, wait patiently. If your waiting be more the exercise of the spiritual life seeking to know and have more of God, wait patiently. Whether it be in the shorter specific periods of waiting, or as the continuous habit of the soul; rest in the Lord, be still before the Lord, and wait patiently. They that wait on the Lord shall inherit the land.'

'My soul, wait thou only upon God!'

Twelfth Day.*WAITING ON GOD: Keeping His Ways.*

'Wait on the Lord, and keep His way,

And He shalt exalt thee to inherit the land.'--Ps. 37: 34.

IF we desire to find a man whom we long to meet, we inquire where the places and the ways are where he is to be found. When waiting on God, we need to be very careful that we keep His ways; out of these we never can expect to find Him. 'Thou meetest him that rejoices and worketh righteousness; those that remember Thee in Thy ways.' We may be sure that God is never and nowhere to be found but in His ways. And that there, by the soul who seeks and patiently waits, He is always most surely to be found. 'Wait on the Lord, and keep His ways, and He shall exalt thee.'

How close the connection between the two parts of the injunction. 'Wait on the Lord,'--that has to do with worship and disposition; 'and keep His ways,'--that deals with walk and work. The outer life must be in harmony with the inner; the inner must be the inspiration and the strength for the outer. It is our God who has made known His ways in His Word for our conduct, and invites our confidence for His grace and help in our heart. If we do not keep His ways, our waiting on Him can bring no blessing. The surrender to a full obedience to all His will, is the secret of full access to all the blessings of His fellowship.

Notice how strongly this comes out in the psalm. It speaks of the evildoer who prospers in his way, and calls on the believer not to fret himself. When we see men around us prosperous and happy while they forsake God's ways, and ourselves left in difficulty or suffering, we are in danger of first fretting at what appears so strange, and then gradually yielding to seek our prosperity in their path. The psalm says, 'Fret not thyself; trust in the Lord, and do good. Rest in the Lord, and wait patiently for Him; cease from anger, and forsake wrath. Depart from evil, and do good; the Lord forsakes not His saints. The righteous shall inherit the land. The law of his God is in his heart; none of his steps shall slide.' And then follows--the word occurs for the third time in the psalm--'Wait on the Lord, and keep His ways.' Do what God asks you to do; God will do more than you can ask Him to do.

And let no one give way to the fear: I cannot keep His ways; it is this robs us of our confidence. It is true you have not the strength yet to keep all His ways. But keep carefully those for which you have received strength already. Surrender yourself willingly and trustingly to keep all God's ways, in the strength which will come in waiting on Him. Give up your whole being to God without reserve and without doubt; He will prove Himself God to you, and work in you that which is pleasing in His sight through Jesus Christ. Keep His ways, as you know them in the Word. Keep His ways, as nature teaches them, in always doing what appears right. Keep His ways, as Providence points them out. Keep His ways, as the Holy Spirit suggests. Do not think of waiting on God while you say you are not willing to walk in His path. However weak you feel, only be willing, and He who has worked to will, will work to do by His power.

'Wait on the Lord, and keep His ways.' It may be that the consciousness of shortcoming and sin makes our text look more like a hindrance than a help in waiting on God. Let it not be so. Have we not said more than once, the very starting-point and groundwork of this waiting is utter and absolute impotence? Why then not come with everything evil you feel in yourself, every memory of unwillingness, unwatchfulness, unfaithfulness, and all that causes such unceasing selfcondemnation? Put your trust in God's omnipotence, and find in waiting on God your deliverance. Your failure has been owing to only one thing: you sought to conquer and obey in your own strength. Come and bow before God until you learn that He is the God who alone is good, and alone can work any good thing. Believe that in you, and all that nature can do, there is no true power. Be content to receive from God each moment the inworking of His mighty grace and life, and waiting on God will become the renewal of your strength to run in His ways and not be weary, to walk in His paths and never faint. 'Wait on the Lord, and keep His ways' will be command and promise in one.

'My soul, wait thou only upon God!'

Thirteenth Day.*WAITING ON GOD: For more than we know.*

'And now, Lord, what wait I for? My hope is in Thee. Deliver me from all my transgressions.'--Ps. 39:7, 8.

THERE may be times when we feel as if we knew not what we are waiting for. There may be other times when we think we do know, and when it would just be so good for us to realize that we do not know what to ask as we ought. God is able to do for us exceeding abundantly above what we ask or think, and we are in danger of limiting Him, when we confine our desires and prayers to our own thoughts of them. It is a great thing at times to say, as our psalm says: 'And now, Lord, what wait I for?' I scarce know or can tell; this only I can say--'My hope is in Thee.'

How we see this limiting of God in the case of Israel! When Moses promised them meat in the wilderness, they doubted, saying, 'Can God furnish a table in the wilderness? He smote the rock that the water gushed out; can He give bread also? Can He provide flesh for His people?' If they had been asked whether God could provide streams in the desert, they would have answered, Yes. God had done it: He could do it again. But when the thought came of God doing something new, they limited Him; their expectation could not rise beyond their past experience, or their own thoughts of what was possible. Even so we may be limiting God by our conceptions of what He has promised or is able to do. Do let us beware of limiting the Holy One of Israel in our very prayer. Let us believe that every promise of God we plead has a divine meaning, infinitely beyond our thoughts of them. Let us believe that His fulfilment of them can be, in a power and an abundance of grace, beyond our largest grasp of thought. And let us therefore cultivate the habit of waiting on God, not only for what we think we need, but for all His grace and power are ready to do for us.

In every true prayer there are two hearts in exercise. The one is your heart, with its little, dark, human thoughts of what you need and God can do. The other is God's great heart, with its infinite, its divine purposes of blessing. What think you? To which of these two ought the larger place to be given in your approach to Him? Undoubtedly, to the heart of God: everything depends upon knowing and being occupied with that. But how little this is done. This is what waiting on God is meant to teach you. Just think of God's wonderful love and redemption, in the meaning these words must have to Him. Confess how little you understand what God is willing to do for you, and say each time as you pray 'And now, what wait I for?' My heart cannot say. God's heart knows and waits to give. 'My hope is in Thee.' Wait on God to do for you more than you can ask or think.

Apply this to the prayer that follows: 'Deliver me from all my transgressions.' You have prayed to be delivered from temper, or pride, or self-will. It is as if it is in vain. May it not be that you have had your own thoughts about the way or the extent of God's doing it, and have never waited on the God of glory, according to the riches of His glory, to do for you what has not entered the heart of man to conceive? Learn to worship God as the God who does wonders, who wishes to prove in you that He can do something supernatural and divine. Bow before Him, wait upon Him, until your soul realizes that you are in the hands of a divine and almighty worker. Consent not to know what and how He will work; expect it to be something altogether godlike, something to be waited for in deep humility, and received only by His divine power. Let the, 'And now, Lord, what wait I for? My hope is in Thee' become the spirit of every longing and every prayer. He will in His time do His work.

Dear soul, in waiting on God you may often be ready to be weary, because you hardly know what you have to expect. I pray you, be of good courage--this ignorance is often one of the best signs. He is teaching you to leave all in His hands, and to wait on Him alone. 'Wait on the Lord! Be strong, and let your heart take courage. Yea, wait on the Lord.'

'My soul, wait thou only upon God!'

Fourteenth Day. *WAITING ON GOD: The Way to the New Song.*

'I waited patiently for the Lord, and He inclined unto me, and heard my cry. . . . And He hath put a new song in my mouth, even praise unto our God.'--Ps. 40: 1-3.

COME and listen to the testimony of one who can speak from experience of the sure and blessed outcome of patient waiting upon God. True patience is so foreign to our self-confident nature, it is so indispensable in our waiting upon God, it is such an essential element of true faith, that we may well once again meditate on what the word has to teach us.

The word patience is derived from the Latin word for suffering. It suggests the thought of being under the constraint of some power from which we want to be free. At first we submit against our will; experience teaches us that when it is vain to resist, patient endurance is our wisest course. In waiting on God it is of infinite consequence that we not only submit, because we are compelled to, but because we lovingly and joyfully consent to be in the hands of our blessed Father. Patience then becomes our highest blessedness and our highest grace. It honors God, and gives Him time to have His way with us. It is the highest expression of our faith in His goodness and faithfulness. It brings the soul perfect rest in the assurance that God is carrying on His work. It is the token of our full consent that God should deal with us in such a way and time as He thinks best. True patience is the losing of our self-will in His perfect will.

Such patience is needed for the true and full waiting on God. Such patience is the growth and fruit of our first lessons in the school of waiting. To many a one it will appear strange how difficult it is truly to wait upon God. The great stillness of soul before God that sinks into its own helplessness and waits for Him to reveal Himself; the deep humility that is afraid to let its own will or its own strength work aught except as God works to will and to do; the meekness that is content to be and to know nothing except as God gives His light; the entire resignation of the will that only wants to be a vessel in which His holy will can move and mold: all these elements of perfect patience are not found at once. But they will come in measure as the soul maintains its position, and ever again says: 'Truly my soul waiteth upon God; from Him cometh my salvation: He only is my rock and my salvation.'

Have you ever noticed what proof we have that patience is a grace for which very special grace is given, in these words of Paul: 'Strengthened with all might, according to His glorious power, unto all'--what? 'patience and long-suffering with joyfulness.' Yes, we need to be strengthened with all God's might, and that according to the measure of His glorious power, if we are to wait on God in all patience. It is God revealing Himself in us as our life and strength, that will enable us with perfect patience to leave all in His hands. If any are inclined to despond, because they have not such patience, let them be of good courage; it is in the course of our feeble and very imperfect waiting that God Himself by His hidden power strengthens us and works out in us the patience of the saints, the patience of Christ Himself.

Listen to the voice of one who was deeply tried: 'I waited patiently for the Lord, and He inclined unto me, and heard my cry.' Hear what he passed through: 'He brought me up also out of an horrible pit, out of the miry clay, and set my feet upon a rock, and established my goings. And He has put a new song in my mouth, even praise unto our God.' Patient waiting upon God brings a rich reward; the deliverance is sure; God Himself will put a new song into your mouth. O soul! be not impatient, whether it be in the exercise of prayer and worship that you find it difficult to wait, or in the delay in respect of definite requests, or in the fulfilling of your heart's desire for the revelation of God Himself in a deeper spiritual life--fear not, but rest in the Lord, and wait patiently for Him. And if you sometimes feel as if patience is not your gift, then remember it is God's gift, and take that prayer (2 Thess. 3: 5 R.V.): 'The Lord direct your hearts into the patience of Christ.' Into the patience with which you are to wait on God, He Himself will guide you.

'My soul, wait thou only upon God!'

Fifteenth Day.*WAITING ON GOD: For His Counsel.*

'They soon forgot His works: they waited not for His counsel.'--Ps. 106: 13.

THIS is said of the sin of God's people in the wilderness. He had wonderfully redeemed them, and was prepared as wonderfully to supply their every need. But, when the time of need came, 'they waited not for His counsel.' They thought not that the Almighty God was their Leader and Provider; they asked not what His plans might be. They simply thought the thoughts of their own heart, and tempted and provoked God by their unbelief. 'They waited not for His counsel.'

How this has been the sin of God's people in all ages! In the land of Canaan, in the days of Joshua, the only three failures of which we read were owing to this one sin. In going up against Ai, in making a covenant with the Gibeonites, in settling down without going up to possess the whole land, they waited not for His counsel. And so even the advanced believer is in danger from this most subtle of temptations--taking God's word and thinking his own thoughts of them, and not waiting for His counsel. Let us take the warning and see what Israel teaches us. And let us very specially regard it not only as a danger to which the individual is exposed, but as one against which God's people, in their collective capacity, need to be on their guard.

Our whole relation to God is rooted in this, that His will is to be done in us and by us as it is in heaven. He has promised to make known His will to us by His Spirit, the Guide into all truth. And our position is to be that of waiting for His counsel, as the only guide of our thoughts and actions. In our church worship, in our prayer-meetings, in our conventions, in all our gatherings as managers, or directors, or committees, or helpers in any part of the work for God, our first object ought ever to be to ascertain the mind of God. God always works according to the counsel of His will; the more that counsel of His will is sought and found and honoured, the more surely and mightily will God do His work for us and through us.

The great danger in all such assemblies is that in our consciousness of having our Bible, and our past experience of God's leading, and our sound creed, and our honest wish to do God's will, we trust in these, and do not realize that with every step we need and may have a heavenly guidance. There may be elements of God's will, applications of God's word, experiences of the close presence and leading of God, manifestations of the power of His Spirit, of which we know nothing as yet. God may be willing, no, God is willing to open up these to the souls who are intently set upon allowing Him to have His way entirely, and who are willing in patience to wait for His making it known. When we come together praising God for all He has done and taught and given, we may at the same time be limiting Him by not expecting greater things. It was when God had given the water out of the rock that they did not trust Him for bread. It was when God had given Jericho into his hands that Joshua thought the victory over Ai was sure; he now knew what God could do, and waited not for counsel from God. And so, while we think that we know and trust the power of God for what we may expect, we may be hindering Him by not giving time, and not definitely cultivating the habit of waiting for His counsel.

A minister has no more solemn duty than teaching people to wait upon God. Why was it that in the house of Cornelius, when 'Peter spoke these words, the Holy Ghost fell upon all that heard him'? They had said, 'We are here before God to hear all things that are commanded you of God.' We may come together to give and to listen to the most earnest exposition of God's truth with little spiritual profit if there be not the waiting for God's counsel. In all our gatherings we need to believe in the Holy Spirit as the Guide and Teacher of God's saints when they wait to be led by Him into the things which God has prepared, and which the heart cannot conceive.

More stillness of soul to realize God's presence; more consciousness of ignorance of what God's great plans may be; more faith in the certainty that God has greater things to show us; more longing that He Himself may be revealed in new glory: these must be the marks of the assemblies of God's saints, if they would avoid the reproach, 'They waited not for His counsel.'

'My soul, wait thou only upon God!'

Sixteenth Day. *WAITING ON GOD: For His Light in the Heart.*

'I wait for the Lord, my soul doth wait,

And in His word do I hope.

My soul waiteth for the Lord

more than they that watch for the morning:

More than they that watch for the morning.'-- Ps. 130:5, 6.

WITH what intense longing the morning light is often waited for. By the mariners in a shipwrecked vessel; by a benighted traveler in a dangerous country; by an army that finds itself surrounded by an enemy. The morning light will show what hope of escape there may be. The morning may bring life and liberty. And so the saints of God in darkness have longed for the light of His countenance, more than watchmen for the morning. They have said, 'More than watchmen for the morning, my soul waiteth for the Lord.' Can we say that too? Our waiting on God can have no higher object than simply having His light shine on us, and in us, and through us, all the day.

God is Light. God is a Sun. Paul says: 'God has shined in our hearts to give the light.' What light? 'The light of the glory of God, in the face of Jesus Christ.' Just as the sun shines its beautiful, life-giving light on and into our earth, so God shines into our hearts the light of His glory, of His love, in Christ His Son. Our heart is meant to have that light filling and gladdening it all the day. It can have it, because God is our sun, and it is written, 'Your sun shall no more go down forever.' God's love shines on us without ceasing.

But can we indeed enjoy it all the day? We can. And how can we? Let nature give us theanswer. Those beautiful trees and flowers, with all this green grass, what do they do to keep thesun shining on them? They do nothing; they simply bask in the sunshine, when it comes. Thesun is millions of miles away, but over all that distance it sends its own light and joy; and thetiniest flower that lifts its little head upwards is met by the same exuberance of light and blessingas flood the widest landscape. We have not to care for the light we need for our day's work; thesun cares, and provides and shines the light around us all the day. We simply count upon it, andreceive it, and enjoy it.

The only difference between nature and grace is this, that what the trees and the flowers do unconsciously, as they drink in the blessing of the light, is to be with us a voluntary and a loving acceptance. Faith, simple faith in God's word and love, is to be the opening of the eyes, the opening of the heart, to receive and enjoy the unspeakable glory of His grace. And even as the trees, day by day, and month by month, stand and grow into beauty and fruitfulness, just welcoming whatever sunshine the sun may give, so it is the very highest exercise of our Christian life just to abide in the light of God, and let it, and let Him, fill us with the life and the brightness it brings.

And if you ask, but can it really be, that even as naturally and heartily as I recognize and rejoice in the beauty of a bright sunny morning, I can rejoice in God's light all the day? It can, indeed. From my breakfast-table I look out on a beautiful valley, with trees and vineyards and mountains. In our spring and autumn months the light in the morning is exquisite, and almost involuntarily we say, How beautiful! And the question comes, Is it only the light of the sun that is to bring such continual beauty and joy? And is there no provision for the light of God being just as much an unceasing source of joy and gladness? There is, indeed, if the soul will but be still and wait on Him, will only let God shine.

Dear soul! learn to wait on the Lord, more than watchers for the morning. All within you may be very dark; is that not the very best reason for waiting for the light of God? The first beginnings of light may be just enough to discover the darkness, and painfully to humble you on account of sin. Can you not trust the light to expel the darkness? Do believe it will. Just bow, even now, in stillness before God, and wait on Him to shine into you. Say, in humble faith; God is light, infinitely brighter and more beautiful than that of the sun. God is light. The Father, the eternal, inaccessible, and incomprehensible light. The Son, the light concentrated, and embodied, and manifested. The Spirit, the light entering and dwelling and shining in our hearts. God is light, and is here shining on my heart. I have been so occupied with the rushlights of my thoughts and efforts, I have never opened the shutters to let His light in. Unbelief has kept it out. I bow in faith: God's light is shining into my heart. The God of whom Paul wrote, 'God hath shined into our heart,' is my God. What would I think of a sun that could not shine? what shall I think of a God that does not shine? No, God shines! God is light! I will take time, and just be still, and rest in the light of God. My eyes are feeble, and the windows are not clean, but I will wait on the Lord. The light does shine, the light will shine in me, and make me full of light. And I shall learn to walk all the day in the light and joy of God. My soul waits on the Lord, more than watchers for the morning.

'My soul, wait thou only upon God!'

Seventeenth Day.*WAITING ON GOD: In Times of Darkness.*

'I will wait upon the Lord, that hideth His face from the house of Jacob; and I will look for Him.'--Isa. 8: 17.

HERE we have a servant of God, waiting upon Him, not on behalf of himself, but of his people, from whom God was hiding his face. It suggests to us how our waiting upon God, though it commences with our personal needs, with the desire for the revelation of Himself, or of the answer to personal petitions, need not, may not, stop there. We may be walking in the full light of God's countenance, and God yet be hiding His face from His people around us; far from our being content to think that this is nothing but the just punishment of their sin, or the consequence of their indifference, we are called with tender hearts to think of their sad estate, and to wait on God on their behalf. The privilege of waiting upon God is one that brings great responsibility. Even as Christ, when He entered God's presence, at once used His place of privilege and honor as intercessor, so we, no less, if we know what it is really to enter in and wait upon God, must use our access for our less favored brethren. 'I will wait upon the Lord, who hides His face from the house of Jacob.'

You worship with a certain congregation. Possibly there is not the spiritual life or joy either in the preaching or in the fellowship that you could desire. You belong to a Church, with its many congregations. There is so much of error or worldliness, of seeking after human wisdom and culture, of trust in ordinances and observances, that you do not wonder that God hides His face, in many cases, and that there is but little power for conversion or true edification. Then there are branches of Christian work with which you are connected--a Sunday school, a gospel hall, a young men's association, a mission work abroad--in which the feebleness of the Spirit's working appears to indicate that God is hiding His face. You think, too, you know the reason. There is too much trust in men and money; there is too much formality and self-indulgence; there is too little faith and prayer; too little love and humility; too little of the spirit of the crucified Jesus. At times you feel as if things are hopeless; nothing will help.

Do believe that God can help and will help. Let the spirit of the prophet come into you, as you take his words, and set yourself to wait on God, on behalf of His erring children. Instead of the tone of judgment or condemnation, of despondency or despair, realize your calling to wait upon God. If others fail in doing it, give yourself doubly to it. The deeper the darkness, the greater the need of appealing to the one only Deliverer. The greater the self-confidence around you, that knows not that it is poor and wretched and blind, the more urgent the call on you who profess to see the evil and to have access to Him who alone can help, to be at your post, waiting upon God. As often as you are tempted to complain, or to sigh and say ever afresh: 'I will wait on the Lord, who hides His face from the house of Jacob.'

There is a still larger circle--the Christian Church throughout the world. Think of Greek, Roman Catholic, and Protestant churches, and the state of the millions that belong to them. Or think only of the Protestant churches with their open Bible and orthodox creeds. How much nominal profession and formality! how much of the rule of the flesh and of man in the very temple of God! And what abundant proof that God does hide His face!

What are those to do who see and mourn this? The first thing to be done is this: 'I will wait on the Lord, who hides His face from the house of Jacob.' Let us wait on God, in the humble confession of the sins of His people. Let us take time and wait on Him in this exercise. Let us wait on God in tender, loving intercession for all saints, our beloved brethren, however wrong their lives or their teaching may appear. Let us wait on God in faith and expectation, until He shows us that He will hear. Let us wait on God, with the simple offering of ourselves to Himself, and the earnest prayer that He would send us to our brethren. Let us wait on God, and give Him no rest until He make Zion a joy in the earth. Yes, let us rest in the Lord, and wait patiently for Him who now hides His face from so many of His children. And let us say of the lifting up of the light of His countenance we desire for all His people, 'I wait for the Lord, my soul doth wait, and my hope is in His word. My soul waits for the Lord, more than the watchers for the morning, the watchers for the morning.'

'My soul, wait thou only upon God!'

Eighteenth Day.*WAITING ON GOD: To Reveal Himself.*

'And it shall be said in that day,Lo, this is our God;we have waited for Him, and He will save us: THIS IS THE LORD; we have waited for Him, we will rejoice and be glad in His salvation,'--Isa. 25:9.

IN this passage we have two precious thoughts.

The one, that it is the language of God's people who have been unitedly waiting on Him; the other, that the fruit of their waiting has been that God has so revealed Himself, that they could joyfully say, Lo, this is our God: this is the Lord. The power and the blessing of united waiting is what we need to learn.

Note the twice repeated, We have waited for Him.' In some time of trouble the hearts of the people had been drawn together, and they had, ceasing from all human hope or help, with one heart set themselves to wait for their God. Is not this just what we need in our churches and conventions and prayer-meetings? Is not the need of the Church and the world great enough to demand it? Are there not in the Church of Christ evils to which no human wisdom is equal? Have we not ritualism and rationalism, formalism and worldliness, robbing the Church of its power? Have we not culture and money and pleasure threatening its spiritual life? Are not the powers of the Church utterly inadequate to cope with the powers of infidelity and iniquity and wretchedness in Christian countries and in heathendom? And is there not in the promise of God, and in the power of the Holy Spirit, a provision made that can meet the need, and give the Church the restful assurance that she is doing all her God expects of her? And would not united waiting upon God for the supply of His Spirit most certainly seem the needed blessing? We cannot doubt it.

The object of a more definite waiting upon God in our gatherings would be very much the same as in personal worship. It would mean a deeper conviction that God must and will do all; a more humble and abiding entrance into our deep helplessness, and the need of entire and unceasing dependence upon Him; a more living consciousness that the essential thing is, giving God His place of honor and of power; a confident expectation that to those who wait on Him, God will, by His Spirit, give the secret of His acceptance and presence, and then, in due time, the revelation of His saving power. The great aim would be to bring every one in a praying and worshipping company under a deep sense of God's presence, so that when they part there will be the consciousness of having met God Himself, of having left every request with Him, and of now waiting in stillness while He works out His salvation.

It is this experience that is indicated in our text. The fulfilment of the words may, at times, be in such striking interpositions of God's power that all can join in the cry, 'Lo, this is our God; this is the Lord!' They may equally become true in spiritual experience, when God's people in their waiting times become so conscious of His presence that in holy awe souls feel, 'Lo, this is our God; this is the Lord!' It is this, alas, that is too much missed in our meetings for worship. The godly minister has no more difficult, no more solemn, no more blessed task, than to lead his people out to meet God, and, before ever he preaches, to bring each one into contact with Him. 'We are now here in the presence of God' -- these words of Cornelius show the way in which Peter's audience was prepared for the coming of the Holy Spirit. Waiting before God, and waiting for God, and waiting on God, are the one condition of God showing His presence.

A company of believers gathered with the one purpose, helping each other by little intervals of silence, to wait on God alone, opening the heart for whatever God may have of new discoveries of evil, of His will, of new openings in work or methods of work, would soon have reason to say, ' Lo, this is our God; we have waited for Him, He shall save us: this is the Lord ; we have waited for Him, we will be glad and rejoice in His salvation.'

'My soul, wait thou only upon God!'

Nineteenth Day. *WAITING ON GOD: As a God of Judgment.*

'Yea, in the way of Thy judgments, O Lord, have we waited for Thee: . . . for when Thyjudgments are on the earth, the inhabitants of the world learn righteousness.'--Isa. 26:8,9.

'The Lord is a God of judgment: blessed are all they that wait for Him.'--Isa. 30:18.

GOD is a God of mercy and a God of judgment. Mercy and judgment are ever together in His dealings. In the flood, in the deliverance of Israel out of Egypt, in the overthrow of the Canaanites, we ever see mercy in the midst of judgment. Within the inner circle of His own people, we see it too: the judgment punishes the sin, while mercy saves the sinner. Or, rather, mercy saves the sinner, not in spite of, but by means of, the very judgment that came upon his sin. In waiting on God, we must beware of forgetting this: as we wait we must expect Him as a God of judgment.

'In the way of Thy judgments, have we waited for Thee.' That will prove true in our inner experience. If we are honest in our longing for holiness, in our prayer to be wholly the Lord's, His holy presence will stir up and discover hidden sin, and bring us very low in the bitter conviction of the evil of our nature, its opposition to God's law, its impotence to fulfill that law. The words will come true, 'Who may abide the day of His coming, for HE is like a refiner's fire.' 'O that Thou would come down, as when the melting fire burns!' In great mercy God executes, within

59

the soul, His judgments upon sin, as He makes it feel its wickedness and guilt. Many a one tries to flee from these judgments: the soul that longs for God, and for deliverance from sin, bows under them in humility and in hope. In silence of soul it says, 'Arise, O Lord! and let Thine enemies be scattered. In the way of Thy judgments we have waited for Thee.'

Let no one who seeks to learn the blessed art of waiting on God, wonder if at first the attempt to wait on Him only discovers more of his sin and darkness. Let no one despair because unconquered sins, or evil thoughts, or great darkness appear to hide God's face. Was not, in His own Beloved Son, the gift and bearer of His mercy on Calvary, the mercy as if hidden and lost in the judgment? Oh, submit, and sink down deep under the judgment of thine every sin: judgment prepares the way, and breaks out in wonderful mercy. It is written, 'Thou shalt be redeemed with judgment.' Wait on God, in the faith that His tender mercy is working out in you His redemption in the midst of judgment: wait for Him, He will be gracious to thee.

There is another application still, one of unspeakable solemnity. We are expecting God, in the way of His judgments, to visit this earth: we are waiting for Him. What a thought! We know of these coming judgments; we know that there are tens of thousands of our professing Christians who live on in carelessness, and who, if no change come, must perish under God's hand. Oh, shall we not do our utmost to warn them, to plead with and for them, if God may have mercy on them. If we feel our want of boldness, want of zeal, want of power, shall we not begin to wait on God more definitely and persistently as a God of judgment, asking Him so to reveal Himself in the judgments that are coming on our very friends, that we may be inspired with a new fear of Him and them, and constrained to speak and pray as never yet. Verily, waiting on God is not meant to be a spiritual self-indulgence. Its object is to let God and His holiness, Christ and the love that died on Calvary, the Spirit and fire that burns in heaven and came to earth, get possession of us, to warn and rouse men with the message that we are waiting for God in the way of His judgments. O Christian! prove that you really believe in the God of judgment.

'My soul, wait thou only upon God!'

Twentieth Day. *WAITING ON GOD: Who waits on us.*

'And therefore will the Lord wait, that He may be gracious unto you; and therefore will He be exalted, that He may have mercy upon you: for the Lord is a God of judgment: blessed are all they that wait for Him.'--Isa. 30:18

WE must not only think of our waiting upon God, but also of what is more wonderful still, of God's waiting upon us. The vision of Him waiting on us, will give new impulse and inspiration to our waiting upon Him. It will give an unspeakable confidence that our waiting cannot be in vain. If He waits for us, then we may be sure that we are more than welcome; that He rejoices to find those He has been seeking for. Let us seek even now, at this moment, in the spirit of lowly waiting on God, to find out something of what it means: 'Therefore will the Lord wait, that He may be gracious unto you.' We shall accept and echo back the message: 'Blessed are all they that wait for Him.'

Look up and see the great God upon His throne. He is Love--an unceasing and inexpressible desire to communicate His own goodness and blessedness to all His creatures. He longs and delights to bless. He has inconceivably glorious purposes concerning every one of His children, by the power of His Holy Spirit, to reveal in them His love and power. He waits with all the longings of a father's heart. He waits that He may be gracious unto you. And each time you come to wait upon Him, or seek to maintain in daily life the holy habit of waiting, you may look up and see Him ready to meet you, waiting that He may be gracious unto you. Yes, connect every exercise, every breath of the life of waiting, with faith's vision of your God waiting for you.

And if you ask, how is it, if He waits to be gracious, that even after I come and wait upon Him, He does not give the help I seek, but waits on longer and longer? there is a double answer. The one is this: God is a wise husbandman, 'who waits for the precious fruit of the earth, and has long patience for it.' He cannot gather the fruit until it is ripe. He knows when we are spiritually ready to receive the blessing to our profit and His glory. Waiting in the sunshine of His love is what will ripen the soul for His blessing. Waiting under the cloud of trial, that breaks in showers of blessing, is as needful. Be assured that if God waits longer than you could wish, it is only to make the blessing doubly precious. God waited four thousand years, until the fullness of time, before He sent His Son: our times are in His hands: He will avenge His elect speedily: He will make haste for our help, and not delay one hour too long.

The other answer points to what has been said before. The giver is more than the gift; God is more than the blessing; and our being kept waiting on Him is the only way for our learning to find our life and joy in Himself. Oh, if God's children only knew what a glorious God they have, and what a privilege it is to be linked in fellowship with Himself, then they would rejoice in Him, even when He keeps them waiting. They would learn to understand better than ever; 'Therefore will the Lord wait, that He may be gracious unto you.' His waiting will be the highest proof of His graciousness.

'Blessed are all they that wait for Him.' Queen has her ladies-inwaiting. The position is one of subordination and service, and yet it is considered one of the highest dignity and privilege, because a wise and gracious sovereign makes them companions and friends. What a dignity and blessedness to be attendants-in-waiting on the Everlasting God, ever on the watch for every indication of His will or favor, ever conscious of His nearness, His goodness, and His grace! 'The Lord is good to them that wait for Him.' 'Blessed are all they that wait for Him.' Yes, it is blessed when a waiting soul and a waiting God meet each other. God cannot do His work without His and our waiting His time: let waiting be our work, as it is His. And if His waiting be nothing but goodness and graciousness, let ours be nothing but a rejoicing in that goodness, and a confident expectancy of that grace. And let every thought of waiting become to us simply the expression of unmingled and unutterable blessedness, because it brings us to a God who waits that He may make Himself known to us perfectly as the Gracious One.

'My soul, wait thou only upon God!'

Twenty-First Day.*WAITING ON GOD: The Almighty One.*

'They that wait on the Lord shall renew their strength; they shall mount up with eagle wings; they shall run and not be weary; they shall walk and not faint.'--Isa. 40: 31.

WAITING always partakes of the character of our thoughts of the one on whom we wait. Our waiting on God will depend greatly on our faith of what He is. In our text we have the close of a passage in which God reveals Himself as the Everlasting and Almighty One. It is as that revelation enters our soul that the waiting will become the spontaneous expression of what we know Him to be--a God altogether most worthy to be waited upon.

Listen to the words: 'Why sayest thou, O Jacob, my way is hid from the Lord?' Why speakest thou as if God does not hear or help?

'Hast thou not known, hast thou not heard, that the Everlasting One, the Lord, the Creator of the ends of the earth, fainteth not, neither is weary?' So far from it, 'He giveth power to the faint, and to them that have no might He increaseth strength. Even the youths'--'the glory of young men is their strength'--'even the youths shall faint, and the young men shall utterly fall:' all that is accounted strong with man shall come to nought. 'But they that wait on the Lord,' on the Everlasting One, who does not faint, neither is weary, they 'shall renew their strength; they shall mount up with wings as eagles; they shall run and,'-- listen now, they shall be strong with the strength of God, and, even as He, 'shall not be weary; they shall walk and,' even as He, 'not faint.'

Yes, 'they shall mount up with wings as eagles.' You know what eagles' wings mean. The eagle is the king of birds, it soars the highest into the heavens. Believers are to live a heavenly life, in the very Presence and Love and Joy of God. They are to live where God lives; they need God's strength to rise there. To them that wait on Him it shall be given.

You know how the eagles' wings are obtained. Only in one way--by the eagle birth. You are born of God. You have the eagles' wings. You may not have known it: you may not have used them; but God can and will teach you to use them.

You know how the eagles are taught the use of their wings. See yonder cliff rising a thousand feet out of the sea. See high up a ledge on the rock, where there is an eagle's nest with its treasure of two young eaglets. See the mother bird come and stir up her nest, and with her beak push the timid birds over the precipice. See how they flutter and fall and sink toward the depth. See now (Deut. 32: 11) 'how she fluttereth over her young, spreadeth abroad her wings, taketh them, beareth them on her wings,' and so, as they ride upon her wings, brings them to a place of safety. And so she does once and again, each time casting them out over the precipice, and then again taking and carrying them. 'So the Lord alone did lead him.' Yes, the instinct of that eagle mother was God's gift, a single ray of that love in which the Almighty trains His people to mount as on eagles' wings.

He stirs up your nest. He disappoints your hopes. He brings down your confidence. He makes you fear and tremble, as all your strength fails, and you feel utterly weary and helpless. And all the while He is spreading His strong wings for you to rest your weakness on, and offering His everlasting Creator-strength to work in you. And all He asks is that you should sink down in your weariness and wait on Him; and allow Him in His Jehovah-strength to carry you as you ride upon the wings of His Omnipotence.

Dear child of God! I pray you, lift up your eyes, and behold your God! Listen to Him who says that He faints not, neither is weary, who promiseth that you too shall not faint or be weary, who asketh nought but this one thing, that you should wait on Him. And let your answer be, With such a God, so mighty, so faithful, so tender,

'My soul, wait thou only upon God!'

Twenty-Second Day. *WAITING ON GOD: It Certainty of Blessing.*

'Thou shalt know that I am the Lord; for they shall not be ashamed that wait for Me.' --Isa. 49:23.

'Blessed are all they that wait for Him.' --Isa. 30:18.

WHAT promises! How God seeks to draw us to waiting on Him by the most positive assurance that it never can be in vain: 'They shall not be ashamed that wait for Me.' How strange that, though we should so often have experienced it, we are yet so slow of learning that this blessed waiting must and can be as the very breath of our life, a continuous resting in God's presence and His love, an unceasing yielding of ourselves for Him to perfect His work in us. Let us once again listen and meditate, until our heart says with new conviction: 'Blessed are they that wait for Him!' In our sixth day's lesson we found in the prayer of Psalm 25: 'Let none that wait on Thee be ashamed.' The very prayer shows how we fear lest it might be. Let us listen to God's answer, until every fear is banished, and we send back to heaven the words God speaks, Yes, Lord, we believe what You say: 'All they that wait for Me shallnot be ashamed.' 'Blessed are all they that wait for Him.'

The context of each of these two passages points us to times when God's Church was in great straits, and to human eye there was no possibility of deliverance. But God interposes with His word of promise, and pledges His Almighty Power for the deliverance of His people. And it is as the God who has Himself undertaken the work of their redemption, that He invites them to wait on Him, and assures them that disappointment is impossible. We, too, are living in days in which there is much in the state of the Church, with its profession and its formalism, that is indescribably sad. Amid all we praise God for, there is, alas, much to mourn over! Were it not for God's promises we might well despair. But in His promises the Living God has given and bound Himself to us. He calls us to wait on Him. He assureth us we shall not be put to shame. Oh that our hearts might learn to wait before Him, until He Himself reveals to us what His promises mean, and in the promises reveals Himself in His hidden glory! We shall be irresistibly drawn to wait on Him alone. God increase the company of those who say, 'Our soul waiteth for the Lord: He is our Help and our Shield.'

This waiting upon God on behalf of His Church and people will depend greatly upon the place that waiting on Him has taken in our personal life. The mind may often have beautiful visions of what God has promised to do, and the lips may speak of them in stirring words, but these are not really the measure of our faith or power. No; it is what we really know of God in our personal experience, conquering the enemies within, reigning and ruling, revealing Himself in His Holiness and Power in our inmost being, --it is this will be the real measure of the spiritual blessing we expect from Him, and bring to our fellowmen. It is as we know how blessed the waiting on God has become to our own souls, that we shall confidently hope in the blessing to come on the Church around us, and the key-word of all our expectations will be; He hath said: 'All they that wait on Me shall not be ashamed.' From what He has done in us, we shall trust Him to do mighty things around us. 'Blessed are all they that wait for Him.' Yes, blessed even now in the waiting. The promised blessings, for ourselves, or for others, may tarry; the unutterable blessedness of knowing and having Him who has promised, the Divine Blesser, the Living Fountain of the coming blessings, is even now ours. Do let this truth get full possession of your souls, that waiting on God is itself the highest privilege of the creature, the highest blessedness of His redeemed child.

Even as the sunshine enters with its light and warmth, with its beauty and blessing, into every little blade of grass that rises upward out of the cold earth, so the Everlasting God meets, in the greatness and the tenderness of His love, each waiting child, to shine in his heart 'the light of the knowledge of the glory of God in the face of Jesus Christ.' Read these words again, until your heart learns to know what God waits to do to you. Who can measure the difference between the great sun and that little blade of grass? And yet the grass has all of the sun it can need or hold. Do believe that in waiting on God, His greatness and your littleness suit and meet each other most wonderfully. Just how in emptiness and poverty and utter impotence, in humility and meekness and surrender to His will, before His great glory, and be still. As you wait on Him, God draws near. He will reveal Himself as the God who will fulfil mightily His every promise. And let your heart ever again take up the song: 'Blessed are all they that wait for Him.'

'My soul, wait thou only upon God!'

Twenty-Third Day. *WAITING ON GOD: For Unlooked-for Things.*

'For since the beginning of the world men have not heard, nor perceived by the ear, neither hath the eye seen, O God, beside Thee, what He hath prepared for him that waiteth for Him.'--Isa. 64:4.

THE R.V. has: 'Neither hath the eye seen a God beside Thee, which worketh for him that waiteth for Him.' In the A.V. the thought is, that no eye hath seenthe thingwhich God hath prepared. In the R.V. no eye hath seen a God, beside our God, who worketh for him that waiteth for Him. To both the two thoughts are common: that our place is to wait upon God, and that there will be revealed to us what the human heart cannot conceive. The difference is: in the R.V. it isthe God who works, in the A.V. the thing He is to work. In 1 Cor. 2:9, the citation is in regard to the things which the Holy Spirit is to reveal, as in the A.V., and in this meditation we keep to that.

The previous verses, specially from chap. 63:15, refer to the low state of God's people. The prayer has been poured out, 'Look down from heaven.' (ver. 15.) 'Why hast Thou hardened my heart from Thy fear? Return for Thy servants' sake.' (ver. 19.) And 64:1, still more urgent, 'Oh that Thou wouldest rend the heavens, that thou wouldest come down, . . . as when the melting fire burneth, to make Thy name known to Thy adversaries!' Then follows the plea from the past, 'When Thou didst terrible things we looked not for, Thou camest down, the mountains flowed down at Thy presence.' 'For'--this is now the faith that has been

71

awakened by the thought of things we looked not for, He is still the same God--'eye hath not seen beside Thee, O God, what He hath prepared for him that waiteth for Him.' God alone knows what He can do for His waiting people. As Paul expounds and applies it: 'The things of God knoweth no man, save the Spirit of God.' 'But God hath revealed them to us by His Spirit.'

The need of God's people, and the call for God's interposition, is as urgent in our days as it was in the time of Isaiah. There is now, as there was then, as there has been at all times, a remnant that seek after God with their whole heart. But if we look at Christendom as a whole, at the state of the Church of Christ, there is infinite cause for beseeching God to rend the heavens and come down. Nothing but a special interposition of Almighty Power will avail. I fear we have no right conception of what the so-called Christian world is in the sight of God. Unless God comes down 'as the melting fire burneth, to make known His name to His adversaries,' our labors are comparatively fruitless. Look at the ministry--how much it is in the wisdom of man and of literary culture --how little in demonstration of the Spirit and of power. Think of the unity of the body--how little there is of the manifestation of the power of a heavenly love binding God's children into one. Think of holiness--the holiness of Christ-like humility and crucifixion to the world--how little the world sees that they have men among them who live in Christ in heaven, in whom Christ and heaven live.

What is to be done? There is but one thing. We must wait upon God. And what for? We must cry, with a cry that never rests, 'Oh that Thou wouldest rend the heavens and come down, that the mountains might flow down at Thy presence.' We must desire and believe, we must ask and expect, that God will do unlooked-for things. We must set our faith on a God of whom men do not know what He has prepared for them that wait for Him. The wonder-doing God, who can surpass all our expectations, must be the God of our confidence.

Yes, let God's people enlarge their hearts to wait on a God able to do exceeding abundantly above what we can ask or think. Let us band ourselves together as His elect who cry day and night to Him for things men have not seen. He is able to arise and to make His people a name, and a praise in the earth. 'He will wait, that He may be gracious unto you; blessed are all they that wait for Him.'

'My soul, wait thou only upon God!'

Twenty-Fourth Day. *WAITING ON GOD: To Know His Goodness.*

'The Lord is good unto them that wait for Him.' -- Lam. 3:25

'THERE is none good but God.' 'His goodness is in the heavens.' 'Oh how great is Thy goodness, which Thou hast laid up for them that fear Thee ' 'Oh, taste and see that the Lord is good!' And here is now the true way of entering into and rejoicing in this goodness of God-waiting upon Him. The Lord is good--even His children often do not know it, for they wait not in quietness for Him to reveal it. But to those who persevere in waiting, whose souls do wait, it will come true. One might think that it is just those who have to wait who might doubt it. But this is only when they do not wait, but grow impatient. The truly waiting ones will all have to say, 'The Lord is good to them that wait for Him.' Wouldst thou fully know the goodness of God, give thyself more than ever to a life of waiting on Him.

At our first entrance into the school of waiting upon God, the heart is chiefly set upon the blessings which we wait for. God graciously uses our need and desire for help to educate us for something higher than we were thinking of. We were seeking gifts; He, the Giver, longs to give Himself and to satisfy the soul with His goodness. It is just for this reason that He often withholds the gifts, and that the time of waiting is made so long. He is all the time seeking to win the heart of His child for Himself. He wishes that we should not only say, when He bestows the gift, How good is God! but that long ere it comes, and even if it never comes, we should all the time be experiencing: 'It is good that a man should quietly wait': 'The Lord is good to them that wait for Him.'

What a blessed life the life of waiting then becomes, the continual worship of faith, adoring and trusting His goodness. As the soul learns its secret, every act or exercise of waiting just becomes a quiet entering into the goodness of God, to let it do its blessed work and satisfy our every need. And every experience of God's goodness gives the work of waiting new attractiveness, and instead of only taking refuge in time of need, there comes a great longing to wait continually and all the day. And however duties and engagements occupy the time and the mind, the soul gets more familiar with the secret art of always waiting. Waiting becomes the habit and disposition, the very second nature and breath of the soul.

Dear Christian! do you not begin to see that waiting is not one among a number of Christian virtues, to be thought of from time to time, but that it expresses that disposition which lies at the very root of the Christian life? It gives a higher value and a new power to our prayer and worship, to our faith and surrender, because it links us, in unalterable dependence, to God Himself. And it gives us the unbroken enjoyment of the goodness of God: 'The Lord is good to them that wait for Him.'

Let me press upon you once again to take time and trouble to cultivate this so much needed element of the Christian life. We get too much of religion at second hand from the teaching of men. That teaching has great value if, even as the preaching of John the Baptist sent his disciples away from himself to the Living Christ, it leads us to God Himself. What our religion needs is--more of God. Many of us are too much occupied with our work. As with Martha, the very service we want to render the Master separates from Him; it is neither pleasing to Him nor profitable to ourselves. The more work, the more need of waiting upon God; the doing of God's will would then, instead of exhausting, be our meat and drink, nourishment and refreshment and strength. 'The Lord is good to them that wait for Him.' How good none can tell but those who prove it in waiting on Him. How good none can fully tell but those who have proved Him to the utmost.

'My soul, wait thou only upon God!'

Twenty-Fifth Day.*WAITING ON THE LORD: Quietly.*

'It is good that a man should both hope and quietly wait for the salvation of the Lord.'--Lam. 3: 26

'TAKE heed, and be quiet: fear not, neither be faint-hearted.' 'In quietness and in confidence shall be your strength.' Such words reveal to us the close connection between quietness and faith, and show us what a deep need there is of quietness, as an element of true waiting upon God. If we are to have our whole heart turned towards God, we must have it turned away from the creature, from all that occupies and interests, whether of joy or sorrow.

God is a being of such infinite greatness and glory, and our nature has become so estranged from Him, that it needs our whole heart and desires set upon Him, even in some little measure to know and receive Him. Everything that is not God, that excites our fears, or stirs our efforts, or awakens our hopes, or makes us glad, hinders us in our perfect waiting on Him. The message is one of deep meaning: 'Take heed and be quiet;' 'In quietness shall be your strength;' 'It is good that a man should quietly wait.'

How the very thought of God in His majesty and holiness should silence us, Scriptureabundantly testifies.

'The Lord is in His holy temple; let all the earth keep silence before Him' (Hab. 2: 20).

'Hold thy peace at the presence of the Lord God.' (Zeph.

1:7). 'Be silent, O all flesh, before the Lord; for He is raised up out of His holy habitation' (Zech. 2:13).

As long as the waiting on God is chiefly regarded as an end towards more effectual prayer, and the obtaining of our petitions, this spirit of perfect quietness will not be obtained. But when it is seen that the waiting on God is itself an unspeakable blessedness, one of the highest forms of fellowship with the Holy One, the adoration of Him in His glory will of necessity humble the soul into a holy stillness, making way for God to speak and reveal Himself. Then it comes to the fulfilment of the precious promise, that all of self and self-effort shall be humbled: 'The haughtiness of man shall be brought down, and the Lord alone shall be exalted in that day.'

Let everyone who would learn the art of waiting on God remember the lesson: 'Take heed, and be quiet;' 'It is good that a man quietly wait.' Take time to be separate from all friends and all duties, all cares and all joys; time to be still and quiet before God. Take time not only to secure stillness from man and the world, but from self and its energy. Let the Word and prayer be very precious; but remember, even these may hinder the quiet waiting. The activity of the mind in studying the Word, or giving expression to its thoughts in prayer, the activities of the heart, with its desires and hopes and fears, may so engage us that we do not come to the still waiting on the All-Glorious One; our whole being is not prostrate in silence before Him. Though at first it may appear difficult to know how thus quietly to wait, with the activities of mind and heart for a time subdued, every effort after it will be rewarded; we shall find that it grows upon us, and the little season of silent worship will bring a peace and a rest that give a blessing not only in prayer, but all the day.

'It is good that a man should quietly wait for the salvation of the Lord.' Yes, it is good. The quietness is the confession of our impotence, that with all our willing and running, with all our thinking and praying, it will not be done: we must receive it from God. It is the confession of our trust that our God will in His time come to our help--the quiet resting in Him alone. It is the confession of our desire to sink into our nothingness, and to let Him work and reveal Himself. Do let us wait quietly. In daily life let there be in the soul that is waiting for the great God to do His wondrous work, a quiet reverence, an abiding watching against too deep engrossment with the world, and the whole character will come to bear the beautiful stamp: Quietly waiting for the salvation of God.

'My soul, wait thou only upon God!'

Twenty-Sixth Day. *WAITING ON GOD: In Holy Expectancy.*

'Therefore will I look to the Lord; I will wait for the God of my salvation; my God will hear me.'--Micah 7: 7.

HAVE you ever read a beautiful little book, Expectation Corner? If not, get it; you will find in it one of the best sermons on our text. It tells of a king who prepared a city for some of his poor subjects. Not far from them were large storehouses, where everything they could need was supplied if they but sent in their requests. But on one condition--that they should be on the outlook for the answer, so that when the king's messengers came with the gifts they had desired, they should always be found waiting and ready to receive them. The sad story is told of one desponding one who never expected to get what he asked, because he was too unworthy. One day he was taken to the king's storehouses, and there, to his amazement, he saw, with his address on them, all the packages that had been made up for him, and sent. There was the garment of praise, and the oil of joy, and the eye salve, and so much more; they had been to his door, but found it closed; he was not on the outlook. From that time on he understood the lesson Micah would teach us today; 'I will look to the Lord; I will wait for the God of my salvation; my God will hear me.'

We have more than once said: Waiting for the answer to prayer is not the whole of waiting, but only a part. Today we want to take in the blessed truth: It is a part, and a very important one. When we have special petitions, in connection with which we are waiting on God, our waiting must be very definitely in the confident assurance: My God will hear me.' A holy, joyful expectancy is of the very essence of true waiting. And this not only in reference to the many varied requests every believer has to make, but most especially to the one great petition which ought to be the chief thing every heart seeks for itself -- that The Life of God in the soul may have full sway; that Christ may be fully formed within; and that we may be filled to all the fullness of God. This is what God has promised. This is what God's people too little seek, very often because they do not believe it possible. This is what we ought to seek and dare to expect, because God is able and waiting to work it in us.

But God Himselfmust work it. And for this end our working must cease. We must see how entirely it is to be the faith of the operation of God who raised Jesus from the dead-- just as much as the resurrection, the perfecting of God's life in our souls is to be directly His work. And waiting has to become more than ever a tarrying before God in stillness of soul, counting upon Him who raises the dead, and calls the things that are not as though they were.

Just notice how the threefold use of the name of God in our text points us to Himself as the onefrom whom alone is our expectation. 'I will look to The Lord; I will wait for The God of my Salvation; My God will hear me.' Everything that is salvation, everything that is good and holy, must be the direct mighty work of God Himself within us. For every moment of a life in the will of God, there must be the immediate operation of God. And the one thing I have to do is this: to look to the Lord; to wait for the God of my salvation; to hold fast the confident assurance, 'My God will hear me.'

God says: 'Be still, and know that I am God. '

There is no stillness like that of the grave. In thegrave of Jesus, in the fellowship of His death, in death to self with its own will and wisdom, its own strength and energy, there is rest. As we cease from self, and our soul becomes still to God, God will arise and show Himself. 'Be still, and know,' then you shall know 'that I am God.' There is no stillness like the stillness Jesus gives when He speaks, 'Peace, be still.' In Christ, in His death, and in His life, in His perfected redemption, the soul may be still, and God will come in, and take possession, and do His perfect work.

'My soul, wait thou only upon God!'

Twenty-Seventh Day. *WAITING ON GOD: For Redemption.*

'Simeon was just and devout, waiting for the consolation of Israel, and the Holy Ghost was upon him. Anna, a prophetess, . . . spake of Him to all then that looked for redemption in Jerusalem.'--Luke 2: 25, 38.

HERE we have the mark of a waiting believer. Just, righteous in all his conduct; devout, devoted to God, ever walking as in His presence; waiting for the consolation of Israel, looking for the fulfillment of God's promises: and the Holy Ghost was on him. In the devout waiting he had been prepared for the blessing. And Simeon was not the only one. Anna spoke to all that looked for redemption in Jerusalem. This was the one mark, amid surrounding formalism and worldliness, of a godly band of men and women in Jerusalem. They were waiting on God; looking for His promised redemption.

And now that the Consolation of Israel has come, and the redemption has been accomplished, do we still need to wait? We do indeed. But will not our waiting, who look back to it as come, differ greatly from those who looked forward to it as coming? It will, especially in two aspects. We now wait on God in the full power of the redemption: and we wait for its full revelation.

Our waiting is now in the full power of the redemption. Christ spoke, 'In that day you shall know that you are in Me. Abide in Me.' The Epistles teach us to present ourselves to God 'as indeed dead to sin, and alive to God in Christ Jesus,' 'blessed with all spiritual blessings in heavenly places in Christ Jesus.' Our waiting on God may now be in the wonderful consciousness, wrought and maintained by the Holy Spirit within us, that we are accepted in the Beloved, that the love that rests on Him rests on us, that we are living in that love, in the very nearness and presence and sight of God. The old saints took their stand on the word of God, and waited, hoping on that word; we rest on the word too -- but, oh! under what exceeding greater privileges, as one with Christ Jesus. In our waiting on God, let this be our confidence: in Christ we have access to the Father; how sure, therefore, may we be that our waiting cannot be vain.

Our waiting differs also in this, that while they waited for a redemption to come, we see itaccomplished, and now wait for its revelation in us. Christ not only said, Abide in Me, but also I in you. The Epistles not only speak of us in Christ, but of Christ in us, as the highest mystery of redeeming love. As we maintain our place in Christ day by day, God waits to reveal Christ in us, in such a way that He is formed in us, that His mind and disposition and likeness acquire form and substance in us, so that by each it can in truth be said, 'Christ liveth in me.'

My life in Christ up there in heaven and Christ's life in me down here on earth -- these two are the complement of each other. And the more my waiting on God is marked by the living faith I in Christ, the more the heart thirsts for and claims the CHRIST IN ME. And the waiting on God, which began with special needs and prayer, will increasingly be concentrated, as far as our personal life is concerned, on this one thing, Lord, reveal Your redemption fully in me; let Christ live in me.

Our waiting differs from that of the old saints in the place we take, and the expectations we entertain. But at root it is the same: waiting on God, from whom alone is our expectation.

Learn from Simeon and Anna one lesson. How utterly impossible it was for them to do anything towards the great redemption -- towards the birth of Christ or His death. It was God's work. They could do nothing but wait. Are we as absolutely helpless as regards the revelation of Christ in us? We are indeed. God did not work out the great redemption in Christ as a whole, and leave its application in detail to us.

The secret thought that it is so lies at the root of all our feebleness. The revelation of Christ in every individual believer, and in each one the daily revelation, step by step and moment by moment, is as much the work of God's omnipotence as the birth or resurrection of Christ. Until this truth enters and fills us, and we feel that we are just as dependent upon God for each moment of our life in the enjoyment of redemption as they were in their waiting for it, our waiting upon God will not bring its full blessing. The sense of utter and absolute helplessness, the confidence that God can and will do all, -- these must be the marks of our waiting as of theirs. As gloriously as God proved Himself to them the faithful and wonder-working God, He will to us also.

'My soul, wait thou only upon God!'

Twenty-Eighth Day. *WAITING ON GOD: For the Coming of His Son.*

'Be ye yourselves like unto men that wait for their Lord.'-- Luke 3:36.

'Until the appearing of our Lord Jesus Christ, which, in His own time, He shall shew, who is theblessed and only Potentate, the King of kings, and Lord of lords.'--1 Tim. 6:14,15(R.V.).

'Turned to God from idols to serve the living and true God, and to wait for His Son from heaven.'--1 Thess. 1: 9, 10.

WAITING on God in heaven, and waiting for His Son from heaven, these two God has joined together, and no man may put them asunder. The waiting on God for His presence and power in daily life will be the only true preparation for waiting for Christ in humility and true holiness. The waiting for Christ coming from heaven to take us to heaven will give the waiting on God its true tone of hopefulness and joy. The Father who in His own time will reveal His Son from heaven, is the God who, as we wait on Him, prepares us for the revelation of His Son. The present life and the coming glory are inseparably connected in God and in us.

There is sometimes a danger of separating them. It is always easier to be engaged with the religion of the past or the future than to be faithful in the religion of today. As we look to what God has done in the past, or will do in time to come, the personal claim of present duty and

86

present submission to His working may be escaped. Waiting on God must ever lead to waiting for Christ as the glorious consummation of His work; and waiting for Christ must ever remind us of the duty of waiting upon God, as our only proof that the waiting for Christ is in spirit and in truth. There is such a danger of our being so occupied with the things that are coming more than with Him who is to come; there is such scope in the study of coming events for imagination and reason and human ingenuity, that nothing but deeply humble waiting on God can save us from mistaking the interest and pleasure of intellectual study for the true love of Him and His appearing. All ye that say ye wait for Christ's coming, be sure that you wait on God now. All ye that seek to wait on God now to reveal His Son in you, see to it that ye do so as men waiting for the revelation of His Son from heaven. The hope of that glorious appearing will strengthen you in waiting upon God for what He is to do in you now: the same omnipotent love that is to reveal that glory is working in you even now to fit you for it.

'The blessed hope and the appearing of the glory of our great God and Savior Jesus Christ,' is one of the great bonds of union given to God's Church throughout the ages. 'He shall come to be glorified in His saints, and to be marveled at in all them that believe.' Then we shall all meet, and the unity of the body of Christ be seen in its divine glory. It will be the meeting-place and the triumph of divine love. Jesus receiving His own and presenting them to the Father. His own meeting Him and worshiping in speechless love that blessed face. His own meeting each other in the ecstasy of God's own love. Let us wait, long for, and love the appearing of our Lord and Heavenly Bridegroom. Tender love to Him and tender love to each other is the true and only bridal spirit.

I fear greatly that this is sometimes forgotten. A beloved brother in Holland was speaking about the expectancy of faith being the true sign of the bride. I ventured to express a doubt. An unworthy bride, about to be married to a prince, might only be thinking of the position and the riches that she was to receive. The expectancy of faith might be strong, and true love utterly wanting. It is love in the bridal spirit. It is not when we are most occupied with prophetic subjects, but when in humility and love we are clinging close to our Lord and His brethren, that we are in the bride's place. Jesus refuses to accept our love except as it is love to His disciples. Waiting for His coming means waiting for the glorious coming manifestation of the unity of the body, while we seek here to maintain that unity in humility and love. Those who love most are the most ready for His coming. Love to each other is the life and beauty of His bride, the Church.

And how is this to be brought about? Beloved child of God! if you would learn aright to wait for His Son from heaven, live even now waiting on God in heaven. Remember how Jesus lived ever waiting on God. He could do nothing of Himself. It was God who perfected His Son through suffering and then exalted Him. It is God alone who can give you the deep spiritual life of one who is really waiting for His Son: wait on God for it. Waiting for Christ Himself is, oh, so different from waiting for things that may come to pass! The latter any Christian can do;

the former, God must work in you every day by His Holy Spirit. Therefore all you who wait on God, look to Him for grace to wait for His Son from heaven in the Spirit which is from heaven. And you who would wait for His Son, wait on God continually to reveal Christ in you.

The revelation of Christ in us as it is given to them who wait upon God is the true preparationfor the full revelation of Christ in glory.

'My soul, wait thou only upon God!'

Twenty-Ninth Day. *WAITING ON GOD: For the Promise of the Father.*

'He charged them not to depart from Jerusalem, but to wait for the promise of the Father.'--Acts 1:4.

IN speaking of the saints in Jerusalem at Christ's birth, with Simeon and Anna, we saw how, though the redemption they waited for is come, the call to waiting is no less urgent now than it was then. We wait for the full revelation in us of what came to them, but what they scarce could comprehend. Even so it is with waiting for the promise of the Father. In one sense, the fulfillment can never come again as it came at Pentecost. In another sense, and that in as deep reality as with the first disciples, we daily need to wait for the Father to fulfil His promise in us.

The Holy Spirit is not a person distinct from the Father in the way two persons on earth are distinct. The Father and the Spirit are never without or separate from each other: the Father is always in the Spirit; the Spirit works nothing but as the Father works in Him. Each moment the same Spirit that is in us, is in God too, and he who is most full of the Spirit will be the first to wait on God most earnestly, further to fulfil His promise, and still strengthen him mightily by His Spirit in the inner man. The Spirit in us is not a power at our disposal. Nor is the Spirit an independent power, acting apart from the Father and the Son. The Spirit is the real living presence and the power of the Father working in us, and therefore it is just he who knows that the Spirit is in him, who will wait on the Father for the full revelation and experience of what the Spirit's indwelling is, for His increase and abounding more and more.

See this in the apostles. They were filled with the Spirit at Pentecost. When they, not long after,on returning from the Council, where they had been forbidden to preach, prayed afresh forboldness to speak in His name--a fresh coming down of the Holy Spirit was the Father's freshfulfillment of His promise.

At Samaria, by the word and the Spirit, many had been converted, and the whole city filled with joy. At the apostles' prayer the Father once again fulfilled the promise. Even so to the waiting company--'We are all here before God'--in Cornelius' house. And so, too, in Acts 13. It was when men, filled with the Spirit, prayed and fasted, that the promise of the Father was afresh fulfilled, and the leading of the Spirit was given from heaven: 'Separate Me Barnabas and Saul.'

So also we find Paul in Ephesians, praying for those who have been sealed with the Spirit, that God would grant them the spirit of illumination. And later on, that He would grant them, according to the riches of His glory, to be strengthened with might by the Spirit in the inner man.

The Spirit given at Pentecost was not a something that God parted with in heaven, and sent away out of heaven to earth. God does not, cannot, give away anything in that way. When He gives grace, or strength, or life, He gives it by giving Himself to work it -- it is all inseparable from

Himself. (See note on Law, The Power of the Spirit, at the end of this volume.) Much more so is the Holy Spirit. He is God, present and working in us: the true position in which we can count upon that working with an unceasing power is as we, praising for what we have, still unceasingly wait for the Father's promise to be still more mightily fulfilled.

What new meaning and promise does this give to our life of waiting! It teaches us ever to keep the place where the disciples tarried at the footstool of the Throne. It reminds us that, as helpless as they were to meet their enemies, or to preach to Christ's enemies, until they were endued with power, we, too, can only be strong in the life of faith, or the work of love, as we are in direct communication with God and Christ, and they maintain the life of the Spirit in us. It assures us that the Omnipotent God will, through the glorified Christ, work in us a power that can bring to pass things unexpected, things impossible. Oh! what will not the Church be able to do when her individual members learn to live their lives waiting on God, and when together, with all of self and the world sacrificed in the fire of love, they unite in waiting with one accord for the promise of the Father, once so gloriously fulfilled, but still unexhausted.

Come and let each of us be still in presence of the inconceivable grandeur of this prospect: the Father waiting to fill the Church with the Holy Ghost. And willing to fill me, let each one say.

With this faith let there come over the soul a hush and a holy fear, as it waits in stillness to take it all in. And let life increasingly become a deep joy in the hope of the ever fuller fulfillment of the Father's promise.

'My soul, wait thou only upon God!'

Thirtieth Day.*WAITING ON GOD: Continually.*

'Therefore turn thou to thy God: keep mercy and judgment, and wait on thy God continually.'--Hos. 12:6.

CONTINUITY is one of the essential elements of life. Interrupt it for a single hour in a man, and it is lost, he is dead. Continuity, unbroken and ceaseless, is essential to a healthy Christian life. God wants me to be, and God waits to make me, I want to be, and I wait on Him to make me, every moment, what He expects of me, and what is well pleasing in His sight. If waiting on God be of the essence of true religion, the maintenance of the spirit of entire dependence must be continuous. The call of God, 'Wait on your God continually,' must be accepted and obeyed. There may be times of special waiting: the disposition and habit of soul must be there unchangeably and uninterrupted.

This waiting continually is indeed a necessity. To those who are content with a feeble Christian life, it appears a luxury something beyond what is essential to being a good Christian. But all who are praying the prayer, 'Lord! make me as holy as a pardoned sinner can be made! Keep me as near to Thee as it is possible for me to be! Fill me as full of Thy love as You are willing to do!' feel at once that it is something that must be had. They feel that there can be no unbroken fellowship with God, no full abiding in Christ, no maintaining of victory over sin and readiness for service, without waiting continually on the Lord.

The waiting continually is a possibility. Many think that

with the duties of life it is out of the question. They cannot be always thinking of it. Even when they wish to, they forget.

They do not understand that it is a matter of the heart, and that what the heart is full of, occupies it, even when the thoughts are otherwise engaged. A father's heart may be filled continuously with intense love and longing for a sick wife or child at a distance, even though pressing business requires all his thoughts. When the heart has learned how entirely powerless it is for one moment to keep itself or bring forth any good, when it has understood how surely and truly God will keep it, when it has, in despair of itself, accepted God's promise to do for it the impossible, it learns to rest in God, and in the midst of occupations and temptations it can wait continually.

This waiting is a promise. God's commands are enablings: gospel precepts are all promises, a revelation of what our God will do for us. When first you begin waiting on God, it is with frequent intermission and frequent failure. But do believe God is watching over you in love and secretly strengthening you in it. There are times when waiting appears to be just losing time, but it is not so. Waiting, even in darkness, is unconscious advance, because it is God you have to do with, and He is working in you. God who calls you to wait on Him, sees your feeble efforts, and works it in you. Your spiritual life is in no respect your own work: as little as you began it, can you continue it; it is God's Spirit who has begun the work in you of waiting upon God; He will enable you to wait continually.

Waiting continually will be met and rewarded by God Himself working continually. We are coming to the end of our meditations. Would that you and I might learn one lesson: God must, God will work continually. He ever does work continually, but the experience of it is hindered by unbelief. But He who by His Spirit teaches you to wait continually, will bring you to experience also how, as the Everlasting One, His work is never-ceasing. In the love and the life and the work of God there can be no break, no interruption.

Do not limit God in this by your thoughts of what may be expected. Do fix your eyes upon this one truth: in His very nature, God, as the only Giver of life, cannot do otherwise than every moment work in His child. Do not look only at the one side: 'If I wait continually, God will work continually.' No, look at the other side. Place God first and say, 'God works continually, every moment I may wait on Him continually.' Take time until the vision of your God working continually, without one moment's intermission, fill your being. Your waiting continually will then come of itself. Full of trust and joy, the holy habit of the soul will be, 'On Thee do I wait all the day.' The Holy Spirit will keep you ever waiting.

'My soul, wait thou only upon God!'

MOMENT BY MOMENT

'I the Lord do keep it: I will water it every moment.'

Dying with Jesus, by death reckoned mine,

Living with Jesus a new life divine;

Looking to Jesus till glory doth shine,

Moment by moment, O Lord, I am Thine.

Chorus--Moment by moment I'm kept in His love,

Moment by moment I've life from above;

Looking to Jesus till glory doth shine;

Moment by moment, O Lord, I am Thine.

Never a battle with wrong for the right, Never a contest that He doth not fight;

Lifting above us His banner so white,

Moment by moment I'm kept in His sight.

Chorus.

Never a trial that He is not there,

Never a burden that He doth not bear,

Never a sorrow that He does not share,

Moment by moment I'm under His care.

Chorus

Never a heartache, and never a groan,

Never a teardrop, and never a moan;

Never a danger but there on the throne

Moment by moment He thinks of His own.

Chorus.

Never a weakness that He doth not feel,

Never a sickness that He cannot heal;

Moment by moment, in woo or in weal,

Jesus, my Savior, abides with me still.

Chorus.

Music in Christian Endeavor Hymns by I. D. Sankey). Or on leaflet by Morgan & Scott

Thirtieth-First Day. *WAITING ON GOD: Only.*

'My soul, wait thou only upon God;

For my expectation is from Him.

He only is my rock and my salvation.'--Isa. 62:5,6.

IT is possible to be waiting continually on God, but not only upon Him; there may be other secretconfidences intervening and preventing the blessing that was expected. And so the word only must come to throw its light on the path to the fullness and certainty of blessing. 'My soul, waitthou only upon God. He only is my Rock.'

Yes, 'My soul, wait thou only upon God.' There is but one God, but one source of life andhappiness for the heart; He only is my Rock; my soul, wait thou onlyupon Him. Thou desirest to be good. 'There is none good but God,' and there is no possible goodness but what is received directly from Him. Thou hast sought to be holy: 'There is none holy but the Lord,' and there is no holiness but what He by His Spirit of holiness every moment breathes in thee. Thou wouldest live and work for God and His kingdom, for men and their salvation. Hear how He says, 'The Everlasting God, the Creator of the ends of the earth. He "alone" fainteth not, neither is weary. He giveth power to the faint, and to them that have no might He increaseth strength. They that wait upon the Lord shall renew their strength.' He only is God; He only is thy Rock: 'My soul, wait thou only upon God.'

'My soul, wait thou only upon God.' Thou will not find many who can help you in this. Enough there will be of thy brethren to draw thee to put trust in churches and doctrines, in schemes and plans and human appliances, in means of grace and divine appointments. But, 'My soul, wait thou only upon God Himself.' His most sacred appointments become a snare when trusted in. The brazen serpent becomes Nehushtan; the ark and the temple a vain confidence. Let the Living God alone, none and nothing but He, be thy hope.

'My soul, wait thou only upon God.' Eyes and hands and feet, mind and thought, may have to be intently engaged in the duties of this life; 'My soul, wait thou only upon God.' Thou art an immortal spirit, created not for this world but for eternity and for God. O, my soul! Realize thy destiny. Know thy privilege, and 'wait thou only upon God.' Let not the interest of religious thoughts and exercises deceive you; they very often take the place of waiting upon God. My soul, wait thou, thy very self, your inmost being, with all its power, 'wait thou only upon God.' God is for thee, thou art for God; wait only upon Him.

Yes, 'my soul, wait thou only upon God.' Beware of your two great enemies -- the World and Self. Beware lest any earthly satisfaction or enjoyment, however innocent it appears, keep you back from saying, 'I will go to God, my exceeding joy.' Remember and study what Jesus says about denying self, 'Let a man deny himself.' Tersteegen says: 'The saints deny themselves in everything.' Pleasing self in little things may be strengthening it to assert itself in greater things. 'My soul, wait thou only upon God;' let

Him be all your salvation and all your desire. Say continually and with an undivided heart, 'From Him comes my expectation; He only is my Rock; I shall not be moved.' Whatever be thy spiritual or temporal need, whatever the desire or prayer of thy heart, whatever thy interest in connection with God's work in the Church or the world--in solitude or in the rush of the world, in public worship or other gatherings of the saints, 'My soul, wait thouonlyupon God.' Let your expectations be from Him alone. He only is your Rock.

'My soul, wait thou only upon God.' Never forget the two foundationtruths on which this blessed waiting rests. If ever you are inclined to think this 'waiting only' is too hard or too high, they will recall thee at once. They are: your absolute helplessness; and, the absolute sufficiency of thy God. Oh! enter deep into the entire sinfulness of all that is of self, and think not of letting self have anything to say one single moment. Enter deep into thy utter and unceasing impotence ever to change what is evil in thee, or to bring forth anything that is spiritually good. Enter deep into thy relation of dependence as creature on God, to receive from Him every moment what He gives. Enter deeper still into His covenant of redemption, with His promise to restore more gloriously than ever what thou hadst lost, and by His Son and Spirit to give within you unceasingly, His actual divine Presence and Power. And thus wait upon your God continually and only.

'My soul, wait thou only upon God.' No words can tell, no heart conceive, the riches of the glory of this mystery of the Father and of Christ. Our God, in the infinite tenderness and omnipotence of His love, waits to be our Life and Joy. Oh, my soul! let it be no longer needed that I repeat the words, 'Wait upon God,' but let all that is in me rise and sing: 'Truly my soul waits upon God. On Thee do I wait all the day.'

'MY SOUL, WAIT THOU ONLY UPON GOD!'1

Printed in Great Britain
by Amazon

37523182R00063